"Kristen Strong is an uncommon gem whose gospel-brilliant writing makes Jesus shine."

—Ann Voskamp, *New York Times* bestselling author

"Change is inevitable, but thriving through it is optional. That's why every woman needs this inspiring and insightful message from Kristen Strong. She's a true encourager and helpful guide who will lead you toward hope and a future one word at a time."

—Holley Gerth, *Wall Street Journal* bestselling author

"I was knee-deep in change when I picked up Kristen's book. Our family was facing a crossroads of jobs, relocation, new schools, new friends and *all the feelings* that go with that level of change. So when I got to chapter 3 and Kristen's experienced, tender permission to 'Don't Just Get Over It,' I may have exhaled my tears and inhaled the rest of the book. Kristen doesn't minimize the pain, fear, or worry that comes with change. Like the dear friend that she is, she simply sits in the midst of it with you until you are ready to see the good that God had always planned for you. This book is not just one more way to get over life's hardest changes but a tender companion to help you get through them."

—Lisa-Jo Baker, author of *Surprised by Motherhood* and community manager for (in)courage

"Kristen Strong is a kindred companion for anyone navigating life's changes. In *Girl Meets Change*, Kristen offers a saturated-with-grace conversation about walking through the seasons of life that are disruptive and disorienting. Her understanding voice and hope-filled truths take us by the hand and help us find our way."

—**Leeana Tankersley,** author of *Breathing Room*

"In her book *Girl Meets Change*, Kristen Strong wisely suggests that perhaps the darkness that often accompanies change doesn't mean we've been abandoned but means we're being covered by God's hand. I had never thought of change that way before, and since reading her kind words, my soul has been deeply encouraged in the midst of my own life transitions. The gift Kristen gives is that she takes what we already know in our heads about change and delivers it gently to our hearts."

—**Emily P. Freeman,** *Wall Street Journal* bestselling author

Girl Meets Change

TRUTHS *to* CARRY YOU *through* LIFE'S TRANSITIONS

Kristen Strong

Revell

a division of Baker Publishing Group
Grand Rapids, Michigan

© 2015 by Kristen Strong

Published by Revell
a division of Baker Publishing Group
P.O. Box 6287, Grand Rapids, MI 49516-6287
www.revellbooks.com

Printed in the United States of America

Library of Congress Cataloging-in-Publication Data
Strong, Kristen.
    Girl meets change : truths to carry you through life's transitions / Kristen Strong.
        pages cm
    Includes bibliographical references.
    ISBN 978-0-8007-2439-9 (pbk.)
    1. Christian women—Religious life. 2. Change (Psychology)— Religious aspects—Christianity. 3. Change—Religious aspects— Christianity. I. Title.
    BV4527.S747 2015
    248.8′43—dc23   2015012128

Published in association with William K. Jensen Literary Agency, 119 Bampton Court, Eugene, Oregon 97404.

15 16 17 18 19 20 21   7 6 5 4 3 2 1

To David, my abundantly good man
who first showed me all change
is a grace.

To James, Ethan, and Faith,
three effervescent joys who forever
changed my life for the better.

Contents

Part 3 Adapt: A Heart That Thrives

Foreword

Let's face it: high school and college are teaching us all wrong.

I've been an official adult for twenty years now, and there are three skills I use daily that I was never taught in school: budgeting, saying no with grace, and knowing how to approach change. I can't remember the last time I diagrammed a sentence or applied the Pythagorean theorem. Can you?

Luckily, there are plenty of books and courses on budgeting, and there are teachers on the topic of doing things with intention. But where are all the books and conferences and hashtags about one of the most inevitable things in life that we all face daily: change?

Change isn't something that happens to us that we have to face with tears, anxiety, and binge-watching HGTV. Change is something God uses to get our attention. Our reactions to change shape our life. And we are grown–ups—we can actually choose how we approach, live through, and respond to change.

When it comes to change, it's possible to thrive, even if that change looks like the exact opposite of the path you'd prefer. That's is the message I needed to hear twenty years ago, that's what I need to remember today—and that's exactly what this book is about.

Kristen has been there, done that and is ready to shine the light on the murky future and imperfect, unknown tomorrow that change often brings with it.

If you need to be encouraged that change isn't synonymous with loss but that it brings along its own gifts, this book might be the best money you've ever spent.

If you need a change mentor, you've found her.

If you are wondering what the Pythagorean theorem is, I think it has to do with math.

Myquillyn Smith
moved fourteen times—most involved the ugly cry
author of *The Nesting Place*

Introduction

If you've ever found change to more resemble foe than friend, this book was written for you.

If you've ever resented change for all the craziness it brought into your life, this book was written just for you.

If you've ever believed change pushed your contentment just outside of reach and stole your joy, I want to hug you hard because *sister, I get it.* If you're like me, unwelcome change smacks right into you, demanding your full attention like a relentless preschooler who hasn't learned the word *no.*

When the change is something I've longed for and hoped to see, then I'm all for it. When change comes that's my own idea, then by all means, bring it. But the many forms of change that are not my idea? I don't think so.

I've lived life believing that if it would just stop changing— and asking me to change with it—I would be more content. I've tried to run away from change, or at least ignore it. But change doesn't go away. It sticks close by, begging us to turn our heads and give it our all-consuming attention. I've done that too, although I've not given it favorable attention. I've hollered and waved my arms at it as I've pleaded with God to take it away.

Until one day, beat-up and bloodied from fighting it, I gave up. I gave up the fight and felt the Lord ask me to change my prayer from *God, remove this change from my life* to *God, remove my attitude toward change.*

That was my simple goal in the beginning. If change isn't going away, then I needed my attitude about change to go away. Not only did God faithfully remove my inability to acknowledge and accept change, but he began to show me how to adapt to it.

Not only adapt to it, but thrive because of it rather than in spite of it.

The answers that came weren't neat and tidy but hard fought. I wish I could say I'm a quick learner of new things, but some tests I retake because I don't pass the first time. I often have to relearn the same lesson more than once, and that takes time. But with a new goal tucked inside my heart—a goal to thrive amidst change—I knew the road that was best for me to travel. And that road was paved with brick after brick fashioned with God's faithful promise of *"You can trust me, girl, because I know what I'm doing."*

I believed him, and with time, I believed the change he allowed in my life was for me, not against me.

Sister, maybe in the furthest corners of your heart you hope there is a way for you to thrive amidst change too. But that idea is a little too fairy tale because the reality you stand in today seems too far gone, too hope-gone. Or maybe you've done your best to avoid change, and in spite of making all the safe choices, change finds you anyway.

That's how it all began for me as an eighteen-year-old high school senior.

The gravel poked under my bare feet as I sprinted toward the mailbox at the end of our curved driveway. Reaching it, I opened the creaky brown metal lid as my eyes instantly grasped what I hoped to find: an envelope from the University of Arkansas's music department. I had already been accepted to the university, but this letter would tell me if I won the scholarship I needed to be able to attend there.

Grabbing the cream-colored envelope, I pulled it out of the mailbox and tore it open. Holding my breath, I unfolded the crisp letter with shaky hands and quickly scanned its contents. I exhaled, its refreshing good news washing over me: I had won the scholarship.

I also received favorable mail from Oklahoma State University, the college so ingrained in my soul I practically bled its school color of orange. But attending the University of Arkansas would not only be an opportunity to study at a music school with a stellar reputation, it would also be an opportunity to gently spread my wings a little farther, beyond my home state of Oklahoma. So I told myself that if I received the University of Arkansas scholarship, I would go.

But when I held the ticket to the school in my hands, I wasn't so sure. As time pressed forward, the Oklahoma State option tugged wearily on my sleeve, insisting I pay attention to all the fine things it offered too:

A good music school.

A family legacy of graduates.

And, given its close proximity to my hometown, many built-in friends.

In the end, Oklahoma State won. Saying yes to OSU felt as comfortable and natural as the school's black-and-orange sweatshirt, so I told people I chose OSU because it just felt right. Privately, however, I knew I chose OSU not because going anywhere else felt wrong but because going anywhere else felt new and scary.

And given a choice, this girl didn't do new and scary.

For as long as I can remember, embracing any kind of change that wasn't my own idea came about as naturally as chewing off my own arm. If you could peek through the curtains of my young adulthood, you'd see me wearing a selfish aversion to change like an invisibility cloak. But change is an unavoidable part of life, and handling it is a skill necessary to our well-being. Life and anything that represents life involves movement, and standing rigid against it will only break us. So being the loving parent he is, God gently but firmly urges us toward the uncomfortable places change brings.

It's a lesson I'm learning imperfectly but learning nonetheless.

With a couple decades from that Summer of Indecision in my rearview mirror, I laugh remembering how my "safe" college choice transformed into the open door where predictability and safe choices faded into oblivion. For during my freshman year at Oklahoma State, I fell in love. And not just with any fellow, but with a fellow in the United States Air Force. So with the date of my twenty-first birthday still ink wet on the calendar, I married my good man and in marriage alone received a crash course in flexibility, humility, and accepting a shared supportive role rather than the sole lead role in the story of my life. Throw in the head-spinning realities of the military lifestyle, and rest assured, I learned to adapt to change in a hundred baptism-by-fire kinds of ways.

Obviously, you don't have to be married to someone in the military to have change accompany your story. You may have moved cross-country—or across an ocean—for employment. You may have gone from being a part of a large corporation to being a small business owner. You may have recently married or divorced, lost your home or moved into a new one. Maybe you just knew homeschooling wasn't for you but now find that since the local schools aren't working for your children, home-schooling is indeed what you've been called to do. Perhaps you birthed a new baby and life feels drastically changed, or those babies you birthed have left home to begin their own new lives. Whatever the view of your circumstances, chances are you're dealing with changes on the inside as much as the outside, feeling the pull of the indecisive tide and just doing all you can to not drift to sea.

If this is you today, oh how I understand! Abram from long ago understood too. These words from Genesis 12 give us a picture of perspective:

The LORD had said to Abram, "Go from your country, your people and your father's household to the land I will show you.

> "I will make you into a great nation,
> and I will bless you.
> I will make your name great,
> and you will be a blessing.
> I will bless those who bless you,
> and whoever curses you I will curse;
> and all peoples on earth
> will be blessed through you."

So Abram went, as the Lord had told him. (vv. 1–4)

What was true for Abram then is true for you today: *if God is sending you to a new place, he's sending you with a promise.* Whether you experience transition under your feet, in your heart, or both, the Lord is bringing you to something new for the purpose of blessing you beyond anything you could ever dream for yourself. In the deepest parts of my soul, I know *change is an absolute provision of God's grace.*

Change isn't something to be feared or dreaded. It's just the next step, his next best thing for you.

The problem, however, is this: we know too little of what could be to feel discontent with what is. When change that isn't our own idea comes into our lives, it's easy to hold on white-knuckled to what we already have where we already are.

If God is sending you to a new place, he's sending you with a promise.

After all, it may not be a terrible or unhealthy place. Where we are may be exactly what you imagined for yourself: beautiful, predictable, and reliable. Why rock the boat?

Or maybe the view from where you sit today isn't quite so ideal. Difficult situations still require courage to change. After all, an undesirable familiar place is still familiar, right? Sometimes we'd rather put our arms around unhealthy predictability than take a chance on a better brand-new.

Either way, what if God wants something more for you? If God knows all our *could be's,* perhaps he's divinely orchestrating your life to help you know them too. And in his infinite wisdom, he is moving you in a new direction toward all that could be.

But when we don't see any of this clearly, it's hard to hang on to belief.

It's my fervent prayer that from the first pages onward, this book shows you how to do just that.

I don't have magic formulas. All I know is that the Giver of all good things wouldn't allow you to be in your current environment today unless it brings you to a better tomorrow. If something is happening that you never fathomed—then God is working out something unfathomably good for you and in you. You may not be able to fill in all the puzzle pieces or connect all the dots, but together we can trust God with the parts we don't see. Together, we can trust God to turn our feelings of hope gone to hope *dawn*. Together, we can believe that if he's asking us to plant a stake in new ground, he wants us to pack the same promise he gave Abram:

"I will bless you."

This is his promise for you.
This is his promise for me.
This is his promise for all women.

Together, may we gather hope as we listen, learn, and believe.

PART 1

Acknowledge

The Change and the Loss

1

Change: Up Close and Personal

There are far, far better things ahead than any we leave behind.

C. S. Lewis

My daughter, Faith, stood gussied up in satin and tulle, and she not-so-patiently waited her turn to walk down the aisle as flower girl in our friend's wedding. While I held her hand at the back of the church, I saw the mother of the groom leave the women's restroom, and her expression said she had all the patience in the world for her almost-daughter-in-law to walk down the aisle. Her tears were hovering just below the surface, and her bottom lip quivered. As I made these observations and others, it was obvious this change—her son becoming a husband—was not welcome at that moment. Oh, I'm certain she's found blessings within the change, such as her son marrying a good, Jesus-loving woman. But as she waited to take her turn in the processional, the pain of what felt like losing a son seemed to outweigh the blessings.

Now, did this mama want her son living in her basement for the rest of his life? I doubt it. I believe she knew this was a good change. However, she just wasn't ready for this change right now.

When change hurts, it doesn't feel like a blessing or a provision of God's grace. So we dig in our heels and decide to ignore it or just suffer begrudgingly through it. Yes, if God allows the pain change brings, then he knows the good purpose found in it will exceed the pain felt. But it's hard to see and know this when we are in the middle of the hurting. So what do we do when the pain change brings is here?

We hold the hand of trust, put one foot in front of the other, and walk through it one slow step after another.

Eventually, the time came for that sweet mother to walk down the aisle. She did it trembling, but she did it just the same. She did it believing that despite her feelings, the blessing was to follow.

Married to Change

It's a cold winter day and I'm trying to work on a project, but my mind is on a conversation I recently had with a new friend at a favorite local coffee shop. I keep freeze-framing the moment after she makes a crazy statement to me. As we sit bookending our china cups of tea and plates of lemon bars, she says, "I want to see change differently, but it doesn't come naturally to me like it does you. You're just one of those people who can handle change, and I'm not." I nearly choke on my chai latte before swallowing. I fervently shake my head back and forth so hard my curly hair swings.

I say, "Well, maybe now I handle it better, but it wasn't always that way. Not by a long shot."

I share with her my story about how change was foreign to me until it barreled into my life with hurricane force.

I am a country girl who spent my childhood surrounded by endless blue skies and wide open Oklahoma prairies. I grew up in the same house on a street aptly named O'Neill Lane—my last name and the last name of everyone who claimed that lane as their address. In my little corner of Osage County, I tirelessly played with my sisters Sara and Megan and explored with our neighbor-cousins Jennifer and Emily, always with imagination to spare. When I needed a break from roaming, climbing, or swimming with the family posse, I kept company with books and diaries under one of many open-armed oaks. Friday nights meant sleepovers and watching *My Fair Lady* with Grandma Rea, and Sunday mornings meant church and pot roast with Grandma Mary. No matter which way I looked, comfort reached out its arms in deep roots and familiar ways.

Protection and stability were also warm companions—I had many needs met with little effort on my part. Community came preassembled. I never had to learn to make friends; they were simply always there. I never wondered who to invite to my birthday party or where we would spend Christmas Eve or even where to buy a Mother's Day gift for my mom. The choices didn't change, and I didn't mind the consistency one bit.

When I left for college a mere forty miles away, many friends left with me. I came home on weekends to enjoy loving family, hot food, and easy laundry. While life on the Oklahoma State campus expanded my horizons, it didn't expand them enough for me to feel any deep-level changes inside. From the get-go, Oklahoma State felt like home away from home.

I assumed that if in college I met a boy I was serious about, I would meet one with solid Oklahoma blood who had designs on properly staying put in state. Oh, he might like to travel, but he would always end each journey on the road back home.

As it turns out, I *did* meet a good Oklahoma boy named David Strong, but David most definitely had no desire to stay put. After all, he had already lived in more states (and countries!) than I'd visited. He knew more people across the globe than I knew in my hometown. And while his passport had seen quite a bit of action, there were countless other places he wanted to visit and explore too.

David embraced change, no matter the flavor, as one of the most exciting things ever, as well as a great excuse to learn and experience new things. Meanwhile, I tended to err on the side of comfortable familiarity. When I was in high school, I did crazy things like drive from my home in the country to our nearby town for a late movie with friends. When David was in high school, he did crazy things like drive from Tulsa to Philadelphia to visit a friend. Interstate highways scared me to death, whereas David saw them as a fast pass to Adventureland. That is, unless he could be above the roads in the sky flying gliders, a type of plane *with no engine*. I didn't relish flying in a plane with two good working engines, let alone one that relied on wind currents to keep it airborne.

Other differences between David and me stood out from the beginning. His family was chock-full of military brass, and as

26

warm and welcoming as they were, their family lifestyle was quite the departure from that of my own artsy, free-spirited self. And our college majors could not have been more opposite: David studied electrical engineering in school, whereas I studied music.

When we both saw each other for the first time on a campus sidewalk, we couldn't help but look again. It took ten seconds flat for the analytical, change-loving boy and the artsy, change-averse girl to fall for each other. We were two very different people, but with a smattering of divine superglue, our differences worked together.

So on a humid June evening in Ponca City, Oklahoma, we united hands and hearts in front of the altar in the only church I'd ever known. We exchanged timeless vows, symbolic rings, and knowing smiles, feeling in our core that Jesus had joined two uncommon people for a common good.

True as this was, two people with such diverse backgrounds can't come together successfully unless some form of change is part of the equation. As David and I planned our honeymoon, I received a gentle introduction to this new experience, early proof of how this boy was already enlarging my vision of the world.

Over coffee and tea in a campus coffee shop, David asked me where I'd like to go for our first trip as a married couple. Since we were college students with little money, I assumed the list of possibilities was small. That was fine with me, however, as there were lots of scenic attractions close to home. I mentally shuffled through the options of never-before-seen places before my mind settled on the perfect location: the Arbuckle Wilderness. This popular tourist attraction in southern Oklahoma had drive-through safaris and countless animal exhibits, and I'd always wanted to visit it. I turned to David and said, "How about the Arbuckle Wilderness? I've never been but always wanted to see it."

Blink. Blink.

"The Arbuckle Wilderness?" He grinned big. "Well, I like the Arbuckle Wilderness as much as the next person, but I was thinking maybe somewhere along the coast. After all, you do love the beach, right?"

Now it was my turn to blink at him.

"The beach? Well, yes, I love the beach. But beaches are too far away and too expensive, don't you think?"

He thought for a moment before adding, "Well, they're farther away and more expensive than the Arbuckle Wilderness, but I've been mulling this over, and if I pull some extra shifts at work, we can do it, I think. Are you up for it?"

I emphatically nodded my head up and down, realizing what I considered possible and what David considered possible were two vastly different things.

Of course, there's nothing wrong with honeymooning at the Arbuckle Wilderness or choosing less grand locations for vacations. After twenty-plus years of marriage, we've done more than our fair share of close-by trips or even happy-at-home staycations. My point is, in those early days of dating and marriage, my vision of the world and all the options in it didn't extend far beyond my driveway. I didn't know how to look further or entertain grandiose dreams. It simply never occurred to me to do so, and what I perceived to be possible reflected this. But David knew how, and with money he saved from his college job (as well as a steady diet of ramen noodles), we were able to afford a trip to the Georgia coast and Florida.

We had been home from our honeymoon for five minutes when the time came to pack our belongings for our first cross-country move. And as we loaded suitcases and boxes into our new old car—my grandmother's orange and cream Chrysler Horizon—my experience with change went from gentle to giant. Marrying David didn't just bring about the usual adjustments that come with sharing life with another person. Marrying *David the air force officer* put my exposure to change into overdrive, and I found myself experiencing things I never thought to include in my childhood scheming and dreaming. If my life before marriage had been a comfortable one-room schoolhouse, it now transformed into a classroom of the world.

If I were to search through the files of your life, I feel confident I could find a defining life change or two of your own. Maybe yours was a move and a new lifestyle like mine. Maybe it was something you expected but nonetheless struggled through—like the change my friend Allison encountered when her oldest child left for college. Or maybe it was out of the blue, like the ordinary Tuesday when my friend Sherri was served with "dissolution of marriage" papers. Or when the doctor called Aundrea and informed her she had a dangerous, life-threatening form of cancer.

Whether expected or not, ready or not, here it comes: difficult, unwanted, and trial-inducing change. And with it comes desperate questions, such as, *How am I supposed to make room in my heart for the new realities change brings when I want nothing to do with the change in the first place? How can I live my life well when life feels completely unfamiliar and foreign? Where do I find contentment in the middle of this messy change?*

Finding God with Us

Outside my window, snow falls in heavy flakes pregnant with beauty. Christmas sits on a calendar date not far from today, and I am reminded of how the first Christmas was when the world waited with pregnant anticipation for our Savior's birth. When I flip open the Gospels to read about this, I see proof that change isn't just something God allows but is something he authors.

> "The virgin will be with child and will give birth to a son, and they will call him Immanuel" (which means, "God with us"). (Matt. 1:22–23)

Talk about drastic change!

For the first time ever, God would dwell on this fallen earth with its faltering people. Everything changed so God could be with us like never before.

It's a personal message meant for my life and your life.

Wrapped in that swaddled bundle of a wee babe is this startling truth: sometimes God allows change in our lives so we can have his presence like never before. So perhaps the first step in making room for unwanted change is acknowledging that it's in our life because he wants to be in our life more. And if this is true, then there is indeed purpose in the difficulty and pain change brings.

But in those early days of marriage I was clueless about this and so many other ways change would affect my life. The girl who grew up neck deep in a tribe of family suddenly found herself alone for long stretches, and for the first time ever I had to figure out how to get used to my own company.

I felt this most acutely when it came to friendships. Gone were the days of easy, close-by friends to hang with and lean on. And since we moved every three years, I had to actively seek out new friends on a continual basis. Not only that, but I had to actively seek out new *everything* on a continual basis. Every few years, our family had to start life over in many respects, from a new neighborhood to a new hairdresser to new doctors and schools. Our church home—and our denomination—also changed as our location and family needs changed. Different seasons brought changes in my identity too. After living much of life as Kristen the daughter and friend, I became Kristen the military wife and busy mom. And with no nearby family to rely on as well as a husband who frequently traveled, I felt the stab of doing many things solo—a lone cheerleader, one woman adding dad, aunt, and grandma to her list of roles.

In most cases, all the changes put me in a position to be the first one to initiate all connections. While this was sometimes easy and natural, at other times it made me feel vulnerable and out of place. Still, after I fought the awkwardness enough to do this (and put on my big girl pants in the process), God provided friendship and community. But once I found a decent-sized village of support, the next move would take it away, leaving me with one that was see-through thin. Over and over, I smacked into the same startling reality as I figured things out on my own:

Change is devastatingly lonely.

Lonely, scary, and overwhelming. And often I have kicked and screamed against it enough to make any toddler proud.

What I didn't know then but know now is this: the lonely, quieter space brought by change is a prime opportunity to open our hearts to see exactly what Jesus wants to teach us. Lonely is not an unfamiliar place for Jesus. He experienced loneliness while hanging on the cross when he cried out to his Father, "My God, my God, why have you forsaken me?" (Matt. 27:46). The loneliness, the loss, and everything else change brings has a purpose, and God knows how to best bring good from it all.

Many folks from small towns or who have lived in one place their whole lives listen to God's whispers and push themselves out of their own comfort zones. They don't live their lives hostile to change. They see beyond their driveway into the horizon, just waiting for God to point them in the direction they need to go. I, however, was not one of those people. God had to push me out of my comfort zone because otherwise I wouldn't have pushed myself. If change hadn't so unapologetically showed up on my doorstep, giving me no choice but to go with it, I would have dug in my heels and crossed my arms against it.

If God is close to us amidst change he brings to us, then he is working through it to bring out some positive change in us as well.

Handling change—beginning to see it as a grace rather than a grouse—takes time. But this I know: one of the key times God is closest is during and after change. And if God is close to us amidst change he brings *to* us, then he is working through it to bring out some positive change *in* us as well.

It takes time to maneuver the rough textures and shadowy shades of change that dips its fingers into all parts of our lives. It takes time for our hearts to accept it. But when we do learn to accept it, we see how God uses it to take us from the (Arbuckle) wilderness to our own (beach) paradise.

While I'm not about to get cocky and consider myself a pro at handling change, I have learned to move with it instead of fight it, to see what Jesus wants me to learn in the midst of it. *To see how he wants to draw me closer to him.* And oh, how I want to be closer to him.

No doubt about it: it's scary to leave the familiar, to leave what we know is comfortable. But you know what? While the old things we leave may be familiar, the new things he brings may be fantastic.

Father in heaven, thank you for sending Jesus so my life might hold the boldest example of change meant for our good. Thank you for sending Jesus so I could hold on to your presence like never before. When change comes to the center of my life, help me to center myself in Jesus. Help me not to hide from change but to discover ways you desire to be closer to me during it. In the never-changing, always gracious name of Jesus, amen.

2

The Way Change Moves

> I've learned the hard way that change can push
> us, pull us, rebuke and remake us. It can show us
> who we've become, in the worst ways, and also
> in the best ways.
>
> Shauna Niequist, *Bittersweet*

Every time I see one of those poignant "So God Made a Farmer" commercials, I can't help but think of my extended farming family, especially my cousin John. Two years my senior, John is an endless source of fascination for me. At six feet five inches, he dwarfs most in his vicinity (though, believe it or not, he's not the tallest person in my family). His deep voice resonates through the most boisterous of rooms. John is gifted at farming the land, and his easygoing manner immediately puts others at ease. He is selfless and bighearted as well as confident and capable—a rare combination of a rough 'n' tough John Wayne and a witty, good-natured Jimmy Fallon. His charming, aw-shucks personality is such that regardless of his height, his presence is felt as much as seen.

John never fascinated me more than during the one year we both attended high school together. Even then, whether on the basketball court, in the classroom, or in the fields, he worked harder than a dozen teenagers put together. All that aside, my favorite memory of John that year is of watching him simply walk down the school hallway. He towered above all the other students by inches and inches, so the hallways would part à la the Red Sea every time he walked through them. Everything took a kind of slow motion turn as heads would swing up to look at the giant of a person with the booming voice taking mammoth steps in size 13 shoes. Of course, anyone who knew John knew he was a gentle giant and there was no reason to be afraid of him. But not all my sophomore classmates felt the same, especially those who judged his personality by his physique.

When change comes walking through the middle of our lives, we can feel like the other high school kids did when John walked down the hallway. It can be scary, intimidating, foreboding. As you toss and turn in the midnight hour, you may feel a truckload of unsettling feelings weigh you down. Sure, you may know in your deep places this change is good for you. You may realize that ultimately, it could bring about something that is unfamiliar but truly fantastic. But just to be safe, maybe you should step wide to the side and get the heck out of change's way. If you're like me, you might curl up tiny in a corner and hope it doesn't see you at all.

However, like my cousin John, change isn't something to jump away from or fear. It's something we can walk toward with an assurance of safety. We can look it in the eyes, uncross our arms, and acknowledge it by calling it what it is: God's next best thing for us. We can open our arms toward heaven knowing that this change, no matter how intimidating, is approved by a good, gentle, and gracious God who desires us to see and feel him in our everyday lives.

Change is a part of each person's story as assuredly as the sun is a part of each new sunrise. However, the way the sun rays hit your windows differs morning to morning. Sometimes you pull back your curtains and see dawn's early light bold and bright, everything blazed in gilded glory. On those kinds of mornings, possibilities burn brilliant and beautiful.

Change is a part of each person's story.

But sometimes the sun shows up a bit more quietly, hiding behind a shroud of blue-pink or dark gray clouds. We still see everything as it was the day before. But without the burnished light, things appear less hopeful.

Of course, hope *is* still there, even when we can't see it. It waits quietly, easily overlooked next to attention-seeking change. It's there because God is there, reminding our hearts of this truth: *When you're tempted to despair about this change, just reorient your heart's location to me, because I never, ever change.*

Like the unique structure of a sunrise, the way change looks and how each person processes it are different each time. We can better acknowledge and be on friendlier terms with change when we look at the different kinds of change and see the way our own circumstances fit inside the big picture. Doing so also helps us prepare for what is to come.

Usually, change will first come either outwardly or inwardly, and one kind usually leads to the other.

Outward Change First

Marrying David showered me with outward changes first. I lived at a new address in a new state. My stuff and his stuff transformed into *our* stuff. I had another living, breathing person taking residence not only in my space but also in my thoughts and plans. David's career also meant that Uncle Sam had a say in where we lived and what we did. No matter the subject, I could no longer go on my merry way taking only myself into consideration.

While David had resided in my heart for some time, it wasn't until after we got married and started living together that I saw deeper changes take place inside me. Like never before, I discovered what it meant to be a living sacrifice by putting his needs before mine. I couldn't say every knee-jerk thing that entered my mind. (*Note to self: Kristen, you still need to work on this.*) I had to make choices that showed I loved him even when I didn't feel like it. I had to learn what always being *for him* looked like. (*Sigh. See above note to self, Kristen.*) This would be easier if being *for him* didn't sometimes feel like it went against me and my own flesh.

So while marriage first brought changes to my outside environment, it wasn't too long before it changed my heart too.

I love the biblical story of Joseph because it illustrates this in one powerfully dramatic story with more twists and turns than a Six Flags roller coaster. Joseph was one of twelve sons born to the patriarch Jacob (see Gen. 37–50). Not only that, he was the not-so-fair-haired golden boy favorite of Jacob. And since Papa Jacob didn't bother to hide his double portion of favor, Joseph knew he was top dog. So what did Joseph do at every opportunity? Use his VIP status to cause trouble, of course. One way he achieved this was sharing his dreams with his eleven brothers, especially the dreams that showed Joseph in a superior position to them: "Listen to this dream I had: We were binding sheaves of grain out in the field when suddenly my sheaf rose and stood upright, while your sheaves gathered around mine and bowed down to it" (Gen. 37:6–7).

Not exactly the way to win friends and influence brothers, is it? And because Joseph just couldn't keep his mouth closed, he informed his brothers of another dream even more audacious than the first, a dream where "the sun and moon and eleven stars were bowing down to me" (Gen. 37:9). Oh my word. Dreaming of crops bowing down to you is one thing, but now it's the sun, moon, and stars? From the brothers' perspective, that just added insult to injury.

Genesis 37 further describes an elaborate gift Jacob gave only to Joseph: a richly ornamented robe (see v. 3). This beautiful item of clothing undoubtedly proved Jacob's out-of-proportion love for his son. And rather than downplay the colorful coat out of concern for his brothers' feelings, Joseph, strutting enough to make any peacock proud, used it to fuel the fires of jealousy with his competitive brothers.

It didn't take long for his brothers to get sick and tired of Joseph and his arrogant behavior. Not only were they tired of the constant reminders of Joseph's preferred status in the family, but Scripture tells us the brothers hated him (see

Gen. 37:4). Wanting to silence Joseph once and for all, they discussed killing him but settled instead on throwing Joseph into an empty cistern. The brothers sat down for a little picnic lunch, probably within earshot of Joseph's inevitable screams. Before they ate the last bites of their meal, they saw a caravan of Midianite merchants passing through on their way to Egypt. They decided to sell Joseph into slavery (see Gen. 37:25–28). Joseph cried out in protest, perhaps even begging forgiveness for his mistakes. Genesis 42:21 tells us the brothers heard him pleading for his life, but they certainly didn't help. Only Joseph's brother Reuben, who had left the gang and returned in hopes of setting Joseph free, was filled with regret and sorrow when he found his brother gone.

Talk about your transformations. Joseph found himself thrown into circumstances testing the furthest limits of outward change. Golden son to unknown kid. Favorable position to detestable situation. Wealthy family member to penniless servant slave. Best-dressed winner to worst-dressed loser.

What about you? Where are the furthest limits your own change has thrown you to? Deep debt? Deep despair? Unimaginable loneliness? Did you cry out, beg for help, only to hear the rush of wind blowing in the trees? Did it seem that by the time help arrived, it was too late? Hold on to Joseph's story, which is lavish with hope. We will see how his story does not end with him enslaved to unwelcome change. No, we will see his story end with the change bringing freedom in powerful ways.

When your outside circumstances change, your story will not end there.

39

Nope, the story doesn't end low in a pit for Joseph. It doesn't end with his wrists bruised from chains. It doesn't end with his heart broken by betrayal.

And you know what? It won't end there for you either.

When your outside circumstances change—either drastically like Joseph's or in a less dramatic fashion—*your story will not end there*. God won't let a single part of that change go to waste. What looks empty will be filled with healing. He will use it to color every component of your life for the better, right down to your heart.

Inward Change First

From the moment I read the positive pregnancy test, motherhood changed me on the inside—and I'm not just talking morning sickness (read *all day sickness* for yours truly here). Knowing I had two new little souls unfolding inside me made me see the world in new wonderful and terrifying ways.

But then I gave birth to two tiny boys eleven minutes apart, and the moment they left my womb is the moment my heart exploded. Change like that—the kind that turns you inside out—can't help but alter your outside world too. In those first weeks of parenting, I lived the first line of *A Tale of Two Cities*: "It was the best of times, it was the worst of times."

I relished being a new mama. Relished, I tell you. And like all good mamas, I believed my babies were the best things God ever knit together in any womb. For the first time in my life, I knew what it was to cry from sheer happiness. I often burst into spontaneous songs and prayers because with these two little gifts, many days felt like Christmas.

But not everything was super sunshiny.

For example, my sleep was cut in half, if not more. And surprise—sleep deprivation can turn nice gals like me into she-devils. Before our babies were born, I could probably count on one hand the number of genuine fights between my husband and me. After our babies were born, that number increased exponentially. Change came to our travel habits too. We could no longer decide to just up and go somewhere—we had to make like *The Grapes of Wrath* and first load up everything but the kitchen sink. Change also affected our budget, our to-dos, and our expectations.

Since my husband and I experienced fertility issues, we were genuinely shocked on that November afternoon when double lines showed up on a pregnancy test. But true as this was, we were intentionally trying to get pregnant, so the shock wasn't what it could have been. We may not have expected the change, but we were hopeful.

For Mary, the mother of Jesus, the news of impending motherhood *to the Son of God* was both unexpected and beyond anything she dared imagine.

Scripture doesn't detail what she was doing when the angel Gabriel visited her, but he clearly took her by surprise. I can see her in my mind's eye, going about her business kneading dough for bread or sweeping her kitchen floor. She turns around or perhaps simply lifts her head and is startled when she sees a stranger standing in her midst. After Gabriel greets her, Scripture says,

> Mary was greatly troubled at his words and wondered what kind of greeting this might be. But the angel said to her, "Do not be afraid, Mary; you have found favor with God. You

will conceive and give birth to a son, and you are to call him Jesus." (Luke 1:29–31)

Talk about your heart-stopping moment brought on by change.

Mary listened to the angel, and while she had some of her questions answered—such as how a virgin like her could be pregnant in the first place—she had to believe by faith that a lot of the answers would make themselves known eventually. In the meantime, she answered,

> "I am the Lord's servant. . . . May it be to me as you have said." Then the angel left her. (Luke 1:38 NIV 1984)

When Mary said yes to God by accepting this drastic change, she also said yes to a whole lot of uncomfortable change in her outside world. First and foremost, she had to tell her fiancé, Joseph, exactly how she became pregnant. And while Scripture tells us God told Joseph the details of Jesus's conception in a dream, he didn't do so until after Mary had told Joseph first. It's hard to imagine a more difficult and awkward conversation between a young woman and her betrothed.

Not only did Mary risk Joseph's unbelief, but she risked public disgrace and a reputation ruined by those who compared her pregnancy's progress to her anniversary date. In spite of Joseph's corroboration, some people likely chose not to believe. I sometimes wonder if being misunderstood ever caused Mary to wonder if life would have been simpler if she had told God no.

Maybe so, but perhaps Mary also knew that short-term simplicity would only bring long-term difficulty. Jesus came to save his mother too. Perhaps she knew that if God was so clearly guiding her changes on the inside, he was surely going to redeem something beautiful through the outside changes too. She must have clung to the words of God's angel, "for nothing is impossible with God" (Luke 1:37 NIV 1984).

Those same words are ours for the taking too. *Nothing is impossible with God.* Nothing. We all have change that affects us on the inside. Whether a baby or a birthday, a diagnosis or a disease brings about change, know that once again, it will not be the end of your story. Know that to be spared from it might bring short-term simplicity but long-term difficulty.

When inward change tumbles and turns, trust as Mary did that nothing is impossible with God. Trust him enough to say, "May it be to me as you have said" (Luke 1:38 NIV 1984).

The Change Is Not the End

In the introduction, we talked about how we don't mind change as long as it's our idea. When this happens, it feels fresh and exciting. We wear it like a new outfit from the store, the kind that we've had our eye on for a while but only recently purchased because of an awesome price markdown. It's the kind of change that makes us want to twirl in the mirror as our hearts jump with giddy gratitude.

But then there's the kind of change that comes like a fountain pen leaking all over that new outfit. You stop twirling and start panicking, thoughts swirling in your mind:

"No! I want it the way it was before!"

"This will not do!"

"How can I fix this?"

At least that's how I felt the second time the air force told us to move, and I really didn't want to move. After all, I had friends. I had a job I loved with people I adored. I had a great hairdresser (hair is important to me, people) and an awesome church. When David brought home papers detailing our new assignment, I cried and complained. This new assignment would not only remove all those good things, but it would take us straight to the deserts of Albuquerque, New Mexico. Being a green grass loving, deciduous tree adoring girl, I wondered how in the Sam Hill I could thrive in the desert. So, serious as a heart attack, I asked David, "Is there any way we can get out of it?"

David returned my question with a look that said, *You still have no idea how this whole military thing works, do you?*

Well, I *did* understand, but I didn't like it.

And that's how I approach a lot of the change that finds me in spite of the fact I never went looking for it. I balk. I cry. I complain. And I ask God, "Is there any way you can get me out of this?"

And he answers, "Yes, Kristen. I will get you out of it. But the only way out is through."

My sweet father knows this all too well. Diagnosed with multiple sclerosis decades ago, Daddy has lived the hard realities of *the only way out is through.* For years following the diagnosis, Daddy was blessed with minimal side effects from the disease and carried on with life normally. He and Mama took long road trips from their home in Oklahoma to visit us wherever we lived. When our sons and our daughter made him a grandpa, Papa Hoyd tirelessly chased my kids around the house and yard.

But seasons changed and time kept moving and Daddy's symptoms intensified, eventually outrunning the medications used for treatment. In the last few years, Daddy's ability to walk has changed, as have several other things. Always the avid storyteller (and my favorite storyteller, for that matter), Daddy remembers only vague phrases from the periphery of each story.

Over time, the changes MS brought metamorphosed from slow and gradual to fast and glaring. What once was felt only by my daddy is felt and seen by anyone near him. It not only has made us ache for all he endures, it has made us ache because *traveling through hurts*. It hurts our feet, our eyes, and our hearts.

But sitting down, slowing down, and massaging our hearts with trust found in the truth of God's Word helps.

All too often, change brings a truckload of sorrow more than just a fountain pen to a dress. At those times, change feels more like someone took a pair of scissors to your dress, or rather a pair of scissors to your heart. No matter the scope of the trial—no matter where it first

The change is not the end. God's grace and goodness are.

shows up and tears you up—remember, the change is not the end. God's grace and goodness are. Yes, *you make it through by moving through.* Just let your feet do the walking and your heart do the believing.

And just like he did for Joseph and Mary, God will use the change to carefully and purposefully weave his blessings into your life.

Prayer

Dear Father God, when change first shows up in my outside environment and I know it will eventually move inside me, please direct your truths from the pages of Scripture to the pages of my heart. And when the change that churns and moves me visits on the inside first, may I unfold that truth tucked inside my heart so my lips say it and my mind believes it. When the winds of change try to sway me and knock me down, may I stand on the solid foundation of your love and guidance. I love you. Thank you for giving us Jesus, in whose name I pray, amen.

3

Don't Just Get Over It

> God wants us to lament. Complaint doesn't see
> the goodness of the character of God. Lament is
> authentic about the feelings but knows the good-
> ness and benevolence of God.
>
> Ann Voskamp

After change knocks into us and we've had the chance
to pick ourselves back up and smooth out our clothes
and hair, we might handle it by choosing one of two extremes.
On one hand, we entertain the idea of hiding under our beds
and pretending nothing is so different. But more often than
not, I think we are more inclined to scold ourselves for feeling the non–Sunday school approved feelings about change.
We secretly wish we were more robot than flesh and heart so
we could reprogram our brains and bodies to *just get over it*.

We need to be okay with *not* getting over it and give ourselves permission to feel the upheaval.

Stacey Thacker unexpectedly lost her father, and she describes the early grief that resulted from that drastic change this way:

> Somehow in the past week our lives have been in fast-forward and slow motion all at the same time. And honestly, I'm not sure if I'm coming or going. A friend of mine told me about a French word. It is *bouleverser*. It means, "a total upheaval, an upset, an absolute reorientation of the way you saw the world before." She said, "That's what you have ahead of you. I and so many others in the family of Christ will be praying you through the agony, the blur, the chaos as you try to figure out a world without your father in it."
>
> Yes. Yes. Yes. This is where I am. In the blur.[1]

No wonder it feels so unnatural to just get over it. Change brings loss, and with the loss comes upheavals and upsets. We are annoyed at ourselves for not being able to totally move on and see things clearly when in reality we can't because we stand in the blur.

What have been the *bouleversers* from your own change? Like Stacey, maybe you lost a parent or another close loved one. Maybe you lost your husband to another woman or a child to an addiction. Maybe you lost your friend to a misunderstanding or your home to foreclosure. Maybe you're about to lose your ever-lovin' mind over the hand you've been unfairly dealt. Whatever the loss, you find yourself spindly legged and wobbly, not sure what to do about it or who to talk to.

My family and I recently experienced a rather large *bouleverser*, and I have to give myself permission to sink into its upheaval, to give myself the space and grace to reorient myself in the unfamiliar blur.

Not long ago, my husband retired from the United States Air Force after twenty-six years of service. I am thankful the process of retirement from the military is a long one, because it gave me time to process the incredible change this would be. That period of processing the change included many nights of tears and scared questions. Because while our departure from the military life meant holding on to wonderful assurances like facing no more deployments or threats of deployments, it also meant entering into unfamiliar territory known as the civilian sector. While I tried not to wrap up my identity in the military lifestyle, it was impossible not to have its all-encompassing nature seep into the cracks of my life just the same. So the uncertainty and questions came: *Will David be able to find a job in the civilian world? Should we stay in our current town or move? What dental insurance should we use?* And with the questions came a healing and an ability to see why this is indeed God's next best move for our family.

But to be honest, this viewpoint is not my knee-jerk reaction.

I feel the pull to bite my lip and get a grip on the situation, to *just get over it already.* In this particular situation—my husband's career change—no one is sick or dying. Still, I once again find I must die in a way. I must be continually ready to give up the parts of my life that God wants to replace with trust in him, even if what I need to give up are my own expectations and continual need to be in the driver's seat of my life.

Yes, I know. This isn't the first time a family has made a career transition. But you know what? It is the first time *my* family has. And while I know the loss from this change won't appear on CNN or FOX News, it's okay for me to mourn the loss just the same.

Those of us in the Western culture seem to struggle with this more than those from other cultures. We are uncomfortable with speaking emotion, let alone showing it. We want to turn our backs on our messy hearts, caring for them in private if we care for them at all. And if someone should catch a glimpse of our breakdown—find us crying our eyes out in a bathroom and ask us what's wrong? Well, we will apologize till the cows come home for our extreme display of emotion, waving it away with our hand and a dismissive, "I'm fine. I'm fine."

Why must we feel the need to apologize for being human and feeling the emotions that are normal to feel as a result of change?

That's a carbon copy of what I did one day not too long ago, the day I stood over my kitchen sink scrubbing the KitchenAid mixing bowl and other cooking utensils. As is often the case over dinner dishes, my mind wandered to the upcoming schedule for the week, which included information meetings at the local high school for my soon-to-be freshmen twin sons. As I washed remnants of bread dough from the bowl, I made the short trip from High School Street to Empty Nest Way, and tears over boys who were in kindergarten just ten minutes ago spilled down my face into the soapy water.

As I swiped away the tears and memories with the back of my hands, my son James sauntered into the kitchen.

"Mama, are you crying?" he asked, eyebrows drawn together in concern.

I smiled weakly. "No, no." I flipped my hand in a flitting, dismissive wave. "I'm just fine." I quickly changed the subject and asked, "Can I help you with something, baby?"

I'm the one needing help with something, and I don't think I'm the only one.

We resent our humanity and weaknesses and do our best to hide them, and in the process we blow off the state of our own hearts and let the hard stuff change brings simmer in our souls. We don't allow ourselves time to grieve the loss of the way things were before.

This isn't the model Jesus used to deal with change, and this isn't his attitude toward changes that affect us either.

Permission to Be Angry

When the news of Lazarus's death reached Jesus, I would assume the first emotion he felt was sorrow. But it isn't.

> When Mary reached the place where Jesus was and saw him, she fell at his feet and said, "Lord, if you had been here, my brother would not have died."
>
> When Jesus saw her weeping and the Jews who had come along with her also weeping, he was deeply moved in spirit and troubled. (John 11:32–33)

My pastor, Mark Bates, gave an interesting, much more telling translation of the world *troubled*. The word in the original Greek better translates to a word akin to a bull snorting.[2] Bull snorting? Interesting.

As I mentioned in the introduction, I grew up with extended family as neighbors, and that family was dairy farmers. Growing up surrounded by dairy cows and the necessary bull or two, I'm no stranger to the sound of bulls snorting. I can still remember swinging on the blue-and-green swing set in our front yard and hearing the telltale snort accompanied by the guttural bellow of a bull. I sometimes stopped swinging long enough to thank God for the barbed wire fence between my swing set and the bull because a snorting bull was an angry bull, preparing for an attack. And I wanted to be nowhere near striking range of that angry bull.

Back to our passage, the phrase "deeply moved in spirit" (v. 33) can be also translated to mean "outraged in spirit." So why exactly was Jesus angry? Was he angry over the loss of his friend? Angry that Mary was criticizing him?

Jesus was angry at death.

My pastor beautifully explains it this way: as the One who came to conquer death, Jesus took death's temporary victory here personally. Because when his people hurt, he hurts. When his people experience loss, he feels the loss. Our pain never escapes him, and he never trivializes it.[3]

When we sweep our own feelings under the proverbial rug, we are trivializing them. If God doesn't work this way, then he certainly doesn't expect us to either. Whether our loss is as monumental as a loved one dying or something much smaller, Jesus sits and comforts. Loss is loss. Jesus doesn't pull out a measuring stick, hold up our loss next to that of the girl over there, and tell us our own loss isn't what it could be. He sits with us and gives us permission to feel all the feelings, including anger.

No doubt about it: *Jesus takes it personally when difficult change brings us loss.* It outrages him to such a level that he flares his nostrils and snorts over it. So whether your loss looks like your husband passing away from cancer or walking away from your marriage, your son's refusal to speak to you, or your friend's insistence that you did something you didn't, God isn't viewing your loss from a faraway spot. And there's no barbed wire fence between him and the loss we face. He gives us permission to attack it, to feel our anger over it. He helps us face it full on so we are better equipped to step out of the blur and into the belief that we are a little bit closer to thriving through our change.

Permission to Let the Tears Flow

Of course we don't want to sit in grief indefinitely, but we need to give ourselves permission to grieve loss, no matter the magnitude.

Grieving comes before the healing.

The shortest verse of the Bible holds powerful impact: "Jesus wept" (John 11:35). All unassuming nine letters sit in the middle of John 11, and they tell *Grieving comes before the healing* the emotion Jesus felt following his anger at death. Here it is in context:

> "Where have you laid him?" he asked.
>
> "Come and see, Lord," they replied.
>
> Jesus wept.
>
> Then the Jews said, "See how he loved him!" (vv. 34–36)

Our tears point us toward what we love. They also point us in the direction of healing.

As a man born with the same feelings and emotions as you and me, Jesus cries because he's incredibly sad over the loss. But more than that, he cries because he desires to fully enter into the suffering of Mary, Martha, and all those who loved Lazarus.

A few verses later, Jesus publicly prays to God, thanking him for hearing the words of his Son. Then he says in a loud voice, "Lazarus, come out!" (John 11:43). Lazarus, with hands and feet wrapped in grave clothes, does just that.

In this instance, God chose to display his authority through Jesus by bringing Lazarus back to life on earth. And in every instance of change, God desires to bring about healing in one way or another. While the healing doesn't usually look like a life literally raised from the dead, it always looks like God bringing life to something dead, raising goodness from something lost. Are we prepared to wait and believe that Jesus, who cries over death himself, is working to conquer it in any way God asks?

As we wait in trust, we can find comfort in our tears because our tears precede our healing.

Aundrea's Story: When Change Brings Unanswered Questions

Aundrea is a homeschooling mom with two beautiful daughters, and her life is a testimony of living well amidst the unanswered questions change and loss bring.[4] Early in her marriage, she suffered two miscarriages. When she was thirty-two, she received the heartbreaking phone call that her father, an active man only fifty-four years young, died suddenly of a massive heart attack. Her oldest daughter was diagnosed with type 1 diabetes at the tender age of eight. These ordeals brought huge changes to Aundrea's life—both the loss of her endearing father's presence and the naive freedom that comes with healthy children, to name just a couple. But even as Aundrea was no stranger at dealing with difficult changes, she wasn't prepared to handle a new one that brought harsh realities saturating her with the pain of unanswered questions.

On an unassuming day in January, Aundrea reached out her right arm to open the car door, and a mole on her forearm caught her eye. It had been there her entire life, but on this particular day, the mole acutely captured her attention. She went home and told her husband, Bryan, she should probably have it removed.

Even though her doctor believed Aundrea's concern was unwarranted, Aundrea could not shake the feeling that the mole's appearance had changed. Finally, her doctor consented to removing the mole. After debating whether she should remove all of it or just a portion of it, the doctor decided it best to remove the entire mole before sending it to pathology.

A few days later, the pathology report for her mole returned with the diagnosis of metastatic melanoma, one of the most dangerous forms of skin cancer. The cancer wasn't as deep as it could have been, but it was deep enough in Aundrea's skin that it had a high chance of spreading. Aundrea, who was hearing this news within hours of losing a good friend to breast cancer, collapsed in fear. She didn't know a great deal about metastatic melanoma, but she had enough medical training as a former ICU nurse to know it could be deadly.

Aundrea says, "I panicked, thinking of lying in the ground near my friend, leaving all our children motherless, all the parenting and homeschooling duties left to our overworked husbands." For days Aundrea cried and couldn't hold it together, not even in front of her children.

Since melanoma tends to spread into surrounding superficial tissues, Aundrea's surgeon recommended a surgery called "wide resection" to ensure removal of any straggling cancer cells. For any melanoma that is as deep in the skin as Aundrea's, protocol also dictates a lymph node biopsy, so the surgeon also had to remove one lymph node. When the pathology report returned from surgery, the surgeon relayed that a barely there 0.1 millimeter spot showed up on her lymph node. Having never seen a melanoma as small as Aundrea's spread to the lymph system, the surgeon was shocked speechless. After receiving the news over the phone, Aundrea hung up and vomited.

Aundrea was referred to a local oncologist to discuss her options. Since radiation and chemo don't kill melanoma and other kinds of immunotherapy have a very low success rate, her only option—other than doing nothing and hoping it hadn't spread—was to have more lymph nodes removed in case the next node also harbored melanoma cells. But even this brought with it undesirable side effects and still couldn't guarantee that cancerous cells wouldn't show up again.

In spite of having no clear answers and the surgery's negative side effects, Aundrea decided to proceed with surgery. When she put her hand on the phone to schedule it, the phone rang. It was a scheduler from the Melanoma Center in San Francisco, two hours away from where Aundrea lived. He told her he'd just received her chart from one of her doctors and that they were interested in scheduling an appointment with her. Aundrea told him she'd just decided to have the surgery at the hospital near her home rather than two hours away in San Francisco. But the scheduler insisted, saying, "You *absolutely must* come up here and talk to the melanoma team. Then you can decide to stay with your current doctor if you wish, but I insist you come up here first."

Aundrea was taken aback. She thought, *What kind of appointment scheduler says things like that? Weird.* But sensing this could be the way God wanted to provide some definitive answers, she went ahead and scheduled an appointment.

After the melanoma team in San Francisco examined Aundrea, they conferred and gave her the most hopeful news she'd had in weeks: there was a chance the spot on her lymph node was another freckle or mole. For particularly freckled and mole-y people, it's common to have pigmented lesions on internal organs, including lymph nodes. Although the hospital dermatopathologist needed to examine her slides further, Aundrea's heart sang. She drove the whole way home thanking God for this sliver of hopeful news.

However, Aundrea's elation was short-lived.

Two weeks later, a total of six dermatopathologists could not decide what to make of her slides. They brought her slides to still more melanoma specialists to discuss her case. While everyone believed the cells on her lymph node looked like a freckle or mole, they were located on a part of the lymph node where melanoma typically resides. To be safe, they recommended Aundrea have surgery to remove that lymph node and those around it.

Aundrea, crushed and full of despair, wondered if there was some sin in her life for which she was being punished now. She said, "I thought God was sparing me from this. He knew how much I didn't want the surgery, how much I feared the side effects and high risk of infection. Why didn't God reveal clearer answers to the doctors? He knows, so why not share the information?"

She asked God the hard questions out loud.

Because her children were quite young and her husband wanted to eliminate any doubt that other malignant cells were being harbored, Aundrea proceeded with the second surgery. This time, twenty-eight lymph nodes were removed. The incredibly rough recovery required her to wear a drain for nearly two months. Her arm remained in an immovable state for weeks and required physical therapy. Since a nerve had to be severed during surgery, much of Aundrea's arm is still numb.

What's more, none of the twenty-eight nodes showed any sign of melanoma.

A year following her surgery, Aundrea says, "I am still perplexed at why God would not enlighten the San Francisco melanoma team—one of the best in the world—as to what those cells really were. I've been able to let go for the most part, but occasionally it does come back to frustrate me. . . . Some things I won't know this side of heaven."

Frustration indeed. Why did Aundrea have to suffer through a difficult, life-altering procedure only to find no evidence of cancer? Why was she given that sliver of hope before surgery only to have it snatched away?

Aundrea's right. She may never get the answers she desires until she meets Jesus and can ask him in person. And knowing Aundrea, I think that's exactly what she'll do.

Honest Communication in All Directions

One of several reasons I respect Aundrea's authenticity and transparency in telling her story is because she isn't afraid to be honest about her feelings concerning the doubt and hard parts. She doesn't put a Band-Aid over her feelings with pep talks full of clichés. She isn't afraid to acknowledge and feel the obvious.

When Aundrea experiences any unwelcome change, she has a real deal, up and down heart-to-heart with God. She tells him how she truly feels, not what she thinks he wants to hear. And she doesn't shy away from keepin' it real with those safe folks next to her too. So when someone at her side asks, "How are you doing?" she won't necessarily give the obligatory, "Fine." She isn't inclined to grit her teeth, gloss over her messy feelings, and refuse to deal with them. She gets angry and cries just like you and me, and in doing so, she doesn't just get over it. She deals with it.

Aundrea models David in the Bible, the same David who lamented,

> I cry aloud to the LORD;
>   I lift up my voice to the LORD for mercy.
> I pour out before him my complaint;
>   before him I tell my trouble.
>   Psalm 142:1–2

David, the future King of Israel, was not shy or quiet about telling God how he *really* felt. His vertical fits heavenward did not put off God, surprise him, or incite the silent treatment in return. In fact, his honesty thrilled God. It thrilled him to such a degree that David was rewarded by being called a man after God's own heart (see Acts 13:22).

God is thrilled with our honesty too. Authentic communication is a sign that our relationship with him is genuine and close. God wants us to want to be real with him, not hide our feelings or dress them up in sparkly talk. When we show God our wounds, we show him we feel our wounds are safe in his presence. They become the bridge to an even closer relationship. When we quit hiding them, we discover he loves us not in spite of our messy feelings but because of them. He loves us no matter what, and our relationship is strengthened by honest communication.

When Aundrea feels God's answers hang back, she makes the hard choice to believe his promises. She says, "I try not to dwell on the fact that the cancer may return, because that steals my joy. All in all, I am most grateful that I was able to return to my regular life with only a few hiccups." Aundrea also counts all the ways God directed her and her physicians to make critical, potentially lifesaving decisions along the way, like that early decision to remove all instead of part of the mole. She sees God's hand on her treatment and recovery even as she wishes he would have provided more concrete answers along the way.

> *When we show God our wounds, we show him we feel our wounds are safe in his presence.*

Like Aundrea, we also need to dwell on the facts of our faith rather than our wobbly feelings. We hold on to the facts of our faith by keeping honest communication both vertically with God and horizontally with safe people in our lives. Throughout the process and afterwards, we give ourselves permission to grieve those losses and let the balm of Christ's love fill in the tender places. We remember we are "hard pressed on every side, but not crushed; perplexed, but not in despair; struck down, but not destroyed" (2 Cor. 4:8–9).

We don't say the words of that verse with shrugged shoulders that beg us to just grit our teeth; we hold on to it with shaky fingers, knowing his promises are solid ground.

We are hard pressed, but not crushed.

We are perplexed, but not in despair.

We are struck down, but not destroyed.

It's something that is easier to manage when we keep honest communication in all directions. It's also something easier to manage when we give those loved ones around us the permission to do the same thing.

Faith's Story: When Change Reveals Hidden Truth

We were closing in on the end of a golden Colorado fall day. While my eight-year-old daughter, Faith, participated in gymnastics class, I penned a checklist of all I needed to pack for an upcoming trip to Pennsylvania. I looked up and watched Faith flip over a low bar and land with a straight back on the mat underneath. Faith completed the move like she had done a hundred times before, landing exactly like she was supposed to. It took only a moment for me to see that while she had landed correctly, something wasn't right. As I leaned in to the observation glass to get a closer look, I noticed her body shaking with sobs. Just then her coach looked up and waved me down to the gym floor.

After flying down the stairs and running through the gym door, I knelt down beside my splayed-out girl. Faith's doe eyes were wide with fright, and she sobbed as she told us she felt "numb and tingly." Her coach was perplexed, as she didn't fall awkwardly and had landed exactly right. I shook my head, just as dumbfounded as her coach. I leaned up close to her head, my hand pushing back her long, honey-colored ponytail. I asked, "Do you think you can stand up?"

She thought a moment before replying in a shaky voice, "I can try."

Faith's coach and I gently pulled her to her feet with one hand while supporting her under her arms. While she easily put weight on her left foot, she couldn't feel her right. So I stood on her right side, holding both hands as she limped to a bench outside the gym. After resting there for a bit, we walked together out to the car.

In the next several minutes, Faith regained all feeling on the right side of her body and felt completely normal. However, we don't mess around with numb and tingly. After the ER trip, X-rays, and a CT scan, we discovered the critical bone—the odontoid—that protects her spinal cord was malformed. This bone protrudes from the second vertebrae, and the malformation meant part of her spine was not as sheltered as it should have been. Without this extra protection, any jarring of the neck could knock the spine into vertebrae bone. This caused the tingly and numb sensations. And if it was jarred hard enough, it could cause much, much worse.

In other words, our daughter had a broken neck.

After the ER trip and exhausting evening, I went to bed around 2:30 a.m., sobbing and sick to my stomach, words like *neurosurgeon* and *spinal surgery* churning around and around in my mind.

I lay there in the dark that night, a little shocked over this whiplash-fast change. Twenty-four hours earlier, I believed my daughter the picture of health. That night we learned otherwise. I replayed the words of the ER doctors—all three sets of them—when they told Faith one by one, "Wow. You're lucky to be alive."

They stuck like barbed wire around my insides, and it hurt to breathe.

My husband crawled into bed next to me and swung one solid arm around my waist. He pulled me close and said in my ear, "Thank you, God, for bringing hidden truth to light."

And I couldn't get over it, couldn't deny it, even as I wished this change wasn't so. God used change to bring hidden truth to light, and I cried with gratitude.

The weeks between Faith's diagnosis and surgery both dragged on and flew by. One thing you need to know about Faith is that she's tremendously active and has more energy than twelve boys put together. That all changed when we discovered her broken neck. The following weeks crawled for her as her movement was placed on extreme restriction. Playing on the jungle gym at school? Nope. Riding her bike around the neighborhood? Big nope. She couldn't even walk up and down the stairs of our house without us holding her hand. And as difficult as it was for her to lose so many freedoms, what did she cry the most tears over losing?

Her favorite sport in the world: gymnastics. Because of the nature of her injury and the high level of danger associated with gymnastics, the sport was out for life. That loss hurt the most—more than the months of restricted movement, more than the precarious surgery and painful recovery, and more than the months of wearing a confining neck brace.

Faith had only been taking gymnastics for three years or so, and she was not on a competitive team. But true to her all or nothing personality, Faith loved—really loved—the sport and had dreams of competing one day. Losing it completely devastated her.

Losing a dream hurts in the deepest places.

So we weren't surprised when we spent night after night consoling her before bed—that time when the sadness of what is no more shows itself doubly dark and gloomy. Of course Faith needed to grieve the change, to feel the anger and release the tears. But what did surprise us was just how long the sadness stayed vivid, how long the shadows of what she could no longer participate in stuck close by. Over a year after she took off her neck brace and was declared physically healed, she attended a gymnastics competition of a good friend. While she cheered bravely for her friend during the competition, the car ride home brought fresh tears, and with those tears a longing for what used to be.

I'm not proud of it, but sometimes my husband and I were tempted to get short with our daughter, to tell her to pick herself up by her size 2 black-and-red cowboy boots and move on. But we were both stopped from blowing off her feelings over a lost dream on account of her tender age. The Holy Spirit gave us both a fresh awareness that that is not what God does. He doesn't ask us to *just turn a page and move on*. As his image bearers, we carry personality traits that don't surprise him. He doesn't love us in spite of our tender, sensitive emotions; he loves us because of them. And if one of his daughters feels deeply for the loss of gymnastics, how much more does he feel deeply for us?

The loss change brings is one way love is made visible, and God does not trivialize our pain or set expiration dates on our mourning. Certainly, grief should have a timetable—we can't sit planted in sorrow till the end of our days. But my own timetable looks just like that: *my own*. It doesn't have to look like yours, and yours doesn't have to look like mine. Yes, there is a time for everything, a time to mourn and a time to dance (see Eccles. 3). But in the transition from one to the other, God is patient.

We must also be patient with ourselves.

And we must be patient with our fellow change-grievers too.

Just Get Through It

Now that we are a couple years removed from the accident, I find it interesting that one of the things Faith most loved in this world—gymnastics—is the same avenue through which God chose to show us her serious health condition. If she hadn't been participating in the sport, we may not have ever discovered her broken neck, or at least not for some time. On one hand, gymnastics is the love lost. But on the other, it is the saving

God does not trivialize our pain or set expiration dates on our mourning

grace. In that is joy because gymnastics will always be a part of Faith's story, a loss redeemed. Yes, something our daughter loved was taken away. But God only allowed it because he wanted to put something better in its place, something she didn't even know was missing: a new awareness of his grace and presence.

Friend, you are the magnum opus of God's creation. He cherishes you more than you could comprehend or fathom. When the loss change brings leaves you in a blur, don't just get over it.

Get through it by asking the difficult questions out loud.

Get through it by giving yourself grace amidst the blur.

Get through it by acknowledging the hard feelings while holding on to God's truth.

And remember, he's holding you too.

Prayer

Heavenly Father, when the blur from change billows and I grieve, thank you for your enduring, quiet patience. When I struggle with unanswered questions, help my heart know it's okay to tell you how I really feel. Give my heart safe people who are not turned off by my hard questions. And whether change sheds light on hidden truth now or not until heaven, may I remember that the change is not purposeless and that you hold me through the process. I love you, Lord. In the saving name of Jesus, amen.

PART 2

Accept

God Is Believable

4

Go Ahead and Give Up

Look back and thank God. Look forward and
trust God.

Anonymous

The boxes were loaded in the stretched-out white truck and
traveling somewhere along I-70 east. The house stood
scrubbed sparkly and clean, easily passing the rigid inspection
required before moving from a house on base. Our silver-blue
minivan had a full tank of gas and sat stocked with books on
CD and travel games. It also held enough goldfish and graham
cracker snacks and juice boxes to fill the bellies of a classroom
full of preschoolers, let alone our three little ones. All the signs
of our cross-country move flashed neon bright, but my pale,
gloomy heart remained rooted where we were—with familiar
people, a familiar setting, a familiar *home*.

I hugged the neck of my sister-friend Rebecca who lived across the street, whose home and heart I'd graced and found grace in countless times. I wrapped my arms around Landon and Cora, Rebecca's darling children who felt more like a niece and nephew than the neighborhood kids. We'd already said our good-byes to Rebecca's husband, Ryan, before he deployed to yet another faraway country. I ushered my own tears from my face as I ushered my crying children into the car. It was the twins' fifth birthday, but all the way around, the mood was anything but celebratory. Even fourteen-month-old Faith had picked up on the somber atmosphere and was out of sorts.

Given this move wasn't my first rodeo, it shouldn't have been this hard to leave. Sure, we had made dear friends here, but we had made good friends in other places too. But this family—and others met on Juniper Court—were much more family than friend. I had seen my twins grow from toddlers to preschoolers there. I'd brought my baby daughter home from the hospital there. For the first time, our family found whole community there—families where the wives shared friendship over meals and tears, the husbands drank Guinness and played darts in our garage, and the kids shared Legos, Thomas trains, and the inevitable germs too. All the way around, the friendships born there were real, and leaving them felt like leaving a part of ourselves. I stared down our minivan, fighting the urge to just plant myself in the driveway forever instead of climbing into the driver's seat of our car.

A timely Scripture came to mind: "From one man he made every nation of men, that they should inhabit the whole earth; and he determined the times set for them and the exact places where they should live" (Acts 17:26 NIV 1984).

I pushed myself into the seat of the minivan, and even though I didn't feel ready to accept this change, I could acknowledge that God's hand was in this move. Oh, I could also still acknowledge that this move was incredibly hard. I cried and hugged our friends and told them it wouldn't be the same without them across the cul-de-sac. I told the kids it was okay and normal to be sad for a while. But it was also okay to keep biblical truth tucked inside our hearts as well, truth that said God directed the next place we were to live, not Uncle Sam. Truth that said if God wants our family somewhere else, it's for our ultimate best.

Truth that said while I felt miserable today because of this move, his promise held hope I wouldn't feel miserable forever.

It's the same words I've told Faith when those teary moments over the loss of gymnastics have spilled over her heart. "Baby, I promise you won't feel miserable about the loss forever."

When we make a family trip to Barnes & Noble, we'll drive past the gym where Faith took gymnastics. From her middle row bucket seat in the minivan, she'll notice the route we're driving and say, "Was this the road we took to gymnastics?"

I'll look up to the rearview mirror and meet her eyes. "Yep, baby. It was."

She'll press her lips together and look back out the window. Tears or no tears, there hangs in the air a wishing things were different. Reminders pop up, like on car trips past the gym. Like when she finds an old leotard in her drawer and holds it up in the mirror. Sometimes she gets a little weepy; other times just heavy in spirit.

When those moments come, like this one on the way to Barnes & Noble, I feel prompted to ask, "Are you doing okay, Faith?"

She keeps staring out the window. "Yeah, Mama, I think so."

I tell her it's okay if she's not, that God understands how she feels. I start the Bible verse for her: "I can do all things . . ."

She looks up at me. No eye roll, just a faint sign of belief.

"Through Christ who strengthens me." She is silent for a minute before adding, "I know this, Mama, but it's just hard sometimes."

I smile sympathetically and tell her I know it is and that it's okay to be sad about it still. I remind her that by believing Jesus will see her through this, her heart is accepting it a bit more each day.

But it *is* hard, isn't it?

I look back at the road and am reminded that when we are confronted with difficult change, time doesn't heal all wounds—time with the Healer does. Time with him spent giving up what I think I want for what God knows I need.

Time doesn't heal all wounds—time with the Healer does.

Yes, I have to learn that sometimes giving up is the right thing to do.

We give up by believing in faith that sometimes we are asked to sacrifice good things so God will give us best things.

When we *give up*, we learn to *trust up* and believe like Abraham that God's promises of blessing come after obedience.

We give up when we live by faith, especially in that murky middle that follows change.

Grace for the Murky Middle

Part of moving from acknowledging to accepting the change in our lives is accepting our need to give ourselves grace through the whole process. Yes, we need grace in the early blur, but we need it in the later middle too. We need it in that middle area that's less foggy but still murky in that it seems to drag on with no clear indication of what should be done next.

We spend much of life in the middle after the calm of transitioning from one end to a new beginning. The middle stretches out in shades of mundane and ordinary. For my girl, it looks like the hard, daily choice to accept that gymnastics is no longer a part of her makeup while also accepting that it will take time to find a new passion. For you, it might look like the hard, daily choice to do the next best thing as you wait for peace in your circumstances. But what we all must do is have the faith to know that even as we can't see where the end of the middle is, God is endlessly dedicated to seeing us through it. He rains down grace on us through our middle places, and in that grace his timing heals all wounds.

I love the words author Emily P. Freeman offers about life's middle parts:

> While some seasons of change are more pronounced than others, aren't we always moving from one thing to another, beginning and ending and middling? Life is made of transition and the soul is always processing something. I do well when I remember to leave a little breathing room for the motion.[1]

I'd do well to leave a little breathing room for the motion too. One thing that helps me find space to breathe? Grace. I need to give myself grace during the murky middle. I remember not to hold my breath but rather to breathe in God's life-giving grace and breathe out trust. I breathe in God's peace and breathe out the release found in giving up and trusting up.

Further breathing room is found when I discover it isn't just my heart that struggles with the ability to accept change at any stage. Turns out my brain—and your brain—struggles with the same thing.

Why It's Not Just Our Hearts That Are Resistant to Change

Not long ago, I made a discovery that shocked the livin' daylights out of me. It also provided me with a key component of being able to accept my current season of change. Are you ready for this? Here it comes:

Our brains are actually wired to resist change.

WHAT?!

My jaw still drops to my chest when I read that sentence. In her book *You're Going to Be Okay*, Holley Gerth gives us the meaning behind this physiological truth:

> The brain stem is the most primitive and basic part of your brain. It sits at the base of your skull and has two responsibilities: survival and threat assessment. . . . Also, the brain stem doesn't like change. It's a status quo junkie. So any kind of change sets off the alarm bells—including when you decide to think differently.[2]

In the past, I've always given my head a free pass when it comes to accepting change by blaming my heart as the one who missed the memo. That explains why so much change, even change that isn't dropped in my lap, is hard to accept. It turns out that while my head gets the memo, it *is* resistant to accepting what it says. I don't know about you, but I find it incredibly freeing to learn my dislike for change goes beyond my familiarity-seeking personality. Turns out my brain functions the same way.

In addition to the brain stem, the brain is also composed of two other primary parts: the limbic system, which is in charge of emotion and connection, and the neocortex, which determines our course of action. However, when you are confronted with change, the brain stem can overwhelm the other two parts as it tries to talk you into doing something *right now* to ease the pain change brings. Like a screaming hurt child, it will do whatever it can to convince you to stop the pain right now.

So when the brain stem pushes us to make a super-quick, super-now decision to stop the uncomfortable feelings coming from change, we'll give in. In other words, we'll put off dealing with the problem or ignore it altogether. We'll panic and snap at the loved ones around us. Or if you're me, you'll consider dropping to the crisscross-applesauce position and planting yourself in the driveway of your familiar house in a familiar neighborhood instead of embracing a new home in a new neighborhood.

The more we encounter change and react this way, the more this becomes our natural thought pattern. Holley explains,

> Our thoughts . . . run on automatic based on past experiences and how we've taught ourselves to respond to different situations. Every time you react a certain way, your brain makes a note of it. That mean the thoughts you think most have the strongest tracks, and your mind automatically goes there. When you decide to "renew your mind," it means stepping off the train and switching the tracks. We have to do this again and again. Then at some point, your brain realizes that this is the new normal response, and it goes there automatically.[3]

The more we react poorly to change, the deeper the grooves in those thought patterns become in our brain. The more we allow those grooves to be the boss of us, the more we become inflexible and give in to knee-jerk reactions to every uncomfortable situation. And the further we fall from being able to accept change. But the more we work at reacting in a more positive, healthy way to change, the closer we become to accepting and even thriving through it.

But how do I stop letting old habits and negative reactions to change be the boss of me? I need to stop driving on cruise control where the pavement is and begin traveling on the gravel roads. Maybe I need to off-road it altogether.

I can "renew my mind" and form new trails by learning the art of having a flexible spirit.

A Flexible Spirit

Theodore Roosevelt said, "There can be no life without change . . . and to be afraid of what is different or unfamiliar is to be afraid of life."[4] If we want to not be afraid of life, we need to hold inside us a flexible spirit. While we are called to rest when appropriate, the nature of life itself is movement. We can stand rigid against the movement and break, or we can lean into flexibility by bending and moving with it. But it doesn't come naturally for folks like me. I have to intentionally move the steering wheel of my brain to a new path and be okay with trying a new route.

I have recently started doing yoga, and I must tell you that as far as exercise goes, it is totally my jam. First of all, the atmosphere of mellow music and low lights creates a soothing "nap time for grown-ups" environment. My instructor is kind, warm, and a patient teacher to yoga newbies like me. Finally, even though I'm not the most flexible girl around by a long shot, I am slowly but surely becoming more so. With each passing week, I am able to bend and stretch further than I could before.

But it takes a lot of slow, intentional stretching over a long period of time. It takes a lot of time in the middle when results don't show up bold and obvious.

I was talking to my good friend Rebecca recently when she mentioned offhand that during her daughter Cora's four-hour gymnastics practices, an entire hour is devoted to stretching. A full 25 percent of her practice time is spent lengthening her tissues and therefore helping her joints and muscles fully extend. While I expected competitive gymnasts like Cora to spend a good deal of time stretching, I didn't think it would be a whole quarter of the practice. But in order to advance to the more difficult moves, the gymnast must work on not only flipping and turning but also increasing her range of motion through stretching. Stretching makes those moves easier to master. Not coincidentally, as her skill level increases, so does her flexibility—and vice versa. Stretching helps prepare the muscles for the work they're about to do. It's their warm-up. It's also an important step in preventing injury to the gymnast.

After talking about this with Rebecca, I immediately started thinking about how during times of change, increasing my spiritual muscles would do more than help create a flexible spirit. It would help prevent injury too. How much time do I devote to spiritually stretching my faith?

Not enough.

When change throws me into the splits position, a flexible spirit is what keeps me from a debilitating injury. It keeps my heart healthier, able to more quickly recover from the sting. That doesn't mean I won't feel the pain, but it does mean that I know I will recover from it sooner than I would with an inflexible spirit.

I want to increase my faith's range of motion so when un-expected change or loss finds me, I am protected from its potentially devastating results.

The Bible says this in Jeremiah 31:3 (NIV 1984):

The LORD appeared to us in the past, saying:

> "I have loved you with an everlasting love;
> I have drawn you with loving-kindness.

I close my eyes and picture Jesus asking me, "Kristen, how have I loved you with an everlasting love and drawn you with loving-kindness?" Answering him is one way to stretch my faith and keep a flexible spirit. You and I can both look at our past and see how the Lord has proven himself believable. Then, with eyes of faith, we trust that he will remain believable through this change in the present and the future.

Everlasting Love

When I look up the original Hebrew word for everlasting, which is *olam*, I find something I would expect: it is trans-lated to mean "continuance," "eternal," and "perpetual."[5] But I also discover it means "the most distant point of view" and "what is at or beyond the horizon, a very distant time."[6] It refers to distant time in ancient history as well as future moments. It refers to God's love stretching in both directions of time.

If you consider your own self in the stretch of time, how has God loved you with an everlasting love? What are the moments when the scales have fallen from your eyes and what you believed purely in faith became sight? When what you hoped for was felt and made real? When prayers were answered in bold living color?

So many stand out to me, like carrying twins nearly to term, delivering a healthy daughter, making friends in new towns—even when it took just this side of forever. When I put that in terms of the Hebrew everlasting, or *olam*, and travel back further in ancient time, I can see other memory markers, like when God brought my parents together on a blind date and how he helped my little sister, born prematurely with underdeveloped lungs, grow and thrive.

These and many others stand out as landmarks in time, hand-delivered gifts of grace. Beautiful evidence of God's everlasting love. Of course, there's no sense pretending there are landmarked events that don't have pretty endings, that have not worked out as I would have hoped. We have all had times when we've been shrouded in the mystery of undesirable outcomes. When those enter my thoughts, I remember that while I don't know why they had to happen or turn out the way they did, the God who feels everlasting love for me does. He loves me through all ancient and future time, so whatever circumstances are a part of my story are a part of his everlasting love for me too. His faithfulness born from that everlasting love carries on and on.

When I sit in times of change, I remember I also sit in his everlasting love. I bend every which way to grasp it, and I'm surprised to see I don't fixate on the change as much as move with it. I remember that with this new change also comes the promise of God's presence like never before. I give up my hopes and hold on to his hope.

Loving-Kindness

The original Hebrew word for loving-kindness is *chesed*, and it is translated to mean "goodness," "merciful," and—get this—*"unchanging love."*[7]

Thank you, God, and glory hallelujah!

If God's love for us is unchanging, then his desire to use change to benefit and bless us is unchanging too. If God's love for us is unchanging, then his desire to help us accept change and thrive through it is unchanging too. Yes, it's hard to see that in the early blur and the murky middle. But I can look once again to God's history with me and see how my testimony brims with proof of his unchanging loving-kindness.

That second move I mentioned in chapter 2, the one I asked David to try to get out of? The one that took us to the desert part of the country? Of all the places we've lived, that desert home was my favorite. Not necessarily because of the place (deserts still aren't my thing, although they know how to do a sunset!) but rather because of the people. Our community there sang with robust and healthy life. While it wasn't perfect, it was perfectly real. It perfectly displayed the Lord's faithfulness because in his loving-kindness, he births beautiful blessings from the bleakest environments.

If during the early blur and murky middle of that move you would have told me Albuquerque would end up being my favorite assignment, I would have slapped my knee and laughed like a crazy person. I would have told you that was *impossible*. But then again, God specializes in doing the impossible. And really, that word isn't even in his vocabulary.

Letting my mind's eye stretch back to that specific time God drew me in with loving-kindness helps my spirit flex just a little more. It is a memory and a monument, a part of my testimony. It and other examples of God's loving-kindness will serve to strengthen the story of my future too.

Do the Next Small Thing

My husband and I have been on-again, off-again watchers of the reality show *Survivor* since it first aired well over a decade ago. One thing about this show that always makes me laugh is the part where Jeff Probst, the host, details the award challenges to the different teams, or tribes. From the viewer's perspective, he gives the rundown of several complicated steps the participants will need to accomplish in order to win. Below is one example of a challenge issued by Jeff:

> On my go, both tribes will race through zigzagging pathways and then through a web of coconuts. You must then work together to get all your tribe members over a ten-foot wall. One tribe member will then dig up a machete and use it to chop a series of ropes releasing a bin of coconuts. Three tribe members will then shoot coconuts into your basket. First tribe to get enough coconuts into their basket to raise their tribe flag wins.[8]

What cracks me up is in spite of the usually complex nature of the challenges, the show participants dutifully nod their heads up and down to show they understand after Jeff gives them a run-through. I always wonder, "Did any of the participants need Jeff to explain what they're supposed to do more than once? Did Jeff have to break it down step-by-step? Surely somebody raised their hand at some point and said, 'Um, Jeff? You lost me after coconuts.'"

I assume it's happened over the course of twenty different seasons the show has aired and hundreds of challenges held within those shows. I believe that off camera, he breaks it down, and the contestants are able to then complete the whole challenge step-by-step.

When it comes to our own experiences with change, each monumental challenge is really just several small challenges completed before the next one. It's taking things day by day, even hour by hour. Instead of losing yourself in the overwhelming picture of how different or difficult things are, it's making the choice to give up and trust up in the decision of the moment.

It is easier for me to give up and trust up when I keep the small decisions—not rabid questions—in the entryway of my mind. Rabid questions that come with change try to steal breathing room and turn my mind's wheel back to the well-worn paths of worry. *What are we going to do now? How are we going to handle this?* They act like magnifying glasses on my concerns, making those concerns grow big and my faith shrink. They encourage me to skip ahead several seasons rather than deal with the here and now.

There is a reason God instructs us to not worry about tomorrow. I love how *The Message* translates Jesus's words in Matthew 6:

If God gives such attention to the appearance of wildflowers—
most of which are never even seen—don't you think he'll attend
to you, take pride in you, do his best for you? What I'm trying
to do here is to get you to relax, to not be so preoccupied with
getting, so you can respond to God's *giving*. People who don't
know God and the way he works fuss over these things, but
you know both God and how he works. Steep your life in God-
reality, God-initiative, God-provisions. Don't worry about
missing out. You'll find all your everyday human concerns
are met. (6:30–33 The Message)

God doesn't want us to worry about the tomorrows of
change because he wants us to see
all the ways he's taking care of us
today. He wants us to look in the
rearview mirror and remember all
the ways he's taken care of us in the
past. And he wants us to have eyes
of faith to believe that he will care
for us tomorrow too.

God doesn't want us to worry about the tomorrows of change because he wants us to see all the ways he's taking care of us today.

This is a God-reality for all in
his creation: God pays attention. He
initiates and provides. On that long
ago day when we moved, I steeped
myself in God-reality by giving up
and climbing into the minivan driver's seat. I backed out of
the driveway, wove my way through town, and found the
highway pointed east.

Then and now, I look to the horizon and pray, "I trust you,
God. I will trade my *what is* for what *will be* because you know
what's best *for me*."

Abraham's Story: Trading What Was for What Will Be

Abraham knew a thing or two about giving up the familiar *what was* for a new *what will be*.

We touched on part of Abram's (Abraham's) story in the introduction, noting that he offers a blueprint for how we can biblically maneuver change. Flipping to Genesis in our Bibles, we learn Abram lived in Haran along with generations of his family and mass quantities of servants and possessions. One day, the Lord appeared with the directive to *get up and go*. If Abram obeyed, the Lord promised to bless him.

It would have been easy to stay in Haran. After all, Abram knew his way around that bustling town. He knew where the corner coffee shop was. He knew the best route to get to the home improvement store. Haran wasn't just familiar; it was a familiar home. It would have been easy for Abram to tell God *no thanks* to the adventure, claiming he was too old and too set in his ways to travel.

It also would have been easy to question God about how in the world he could possibly father a nation at seventy-five years of age when he had so far been unable to father a single child.

Instead of giving up on faith-filled possibilities, he gave up his questions and went.

In Genesis 12:1, God tells Abram to go. In Genesis 12:2, he tells him what this change will bring. And in Genesis 12:4, Scripture says, "So Abram went."

Sure enough, Abram obeyed God and left all that was safe and familiar, easy and comfortable. He picked up and went to where God commanded, and through his doing so

God blessed him as the father of generations. The lesson for us as women today is this: when God uses change to send us packing, he sends us with the promise of blessing too.

> Abraham "believed God, and it was credited to him as righteousness." Understand, then, that those who have faith are children of Abraham. Scripture foresaw that God would justify the Gentiles by faith, and announced the gospel in advance to Abraham: "All nations will be blessed through you." So those who rely on faith are blessed along with Abraham, the man of faith. (Gal. 3:6–9)

When we are obedient through change just as Abraham was, God's promises of provision, favor, and blessing are ours as well. He is as committed to us as he was to Abraham. When we hold on to faith and believe this, we see that change is not a life hindrance but a life occurrence acting as a stepping-stone toward his very best for us.

Yes, when God sends people packing, he sends them with a promise of blessing. When God asks us to give up something, it's because he wants to give us something better. Are you being sent packing somewhere today? Is it from a place of security to a place of obscurity? From your home to the hospital bed? From your job to the unemployment line? From the welcoming dinner table of friends to the slammed front door? Or are you helping your child pack his room for his first college dorm or new apartment? Whatever

When God uses change to send us packing, he sends us with the promise of blessing too.

it is—wherever it is—leave room in your heart's suitcase for God's promise of blessing. It may not come today, I know. But on the other hand, it just might show up sooner than you think.

Beth Moore says, "God calls us to leave our familiar spiritual countryside—our ruts, our comfort zones, and every hint of mediocrity—and 'go' to the place he will show us."[9]

Grab your suitcases, girls. God thinks too much of us to let us settle. Let's get ready to roll.

What Giving Up Gives You

It's been a beautiful afternoon, one where I hosted a tea party for some of my friends as well as one of Faith's. Faith helps me clean up the cups and saucers and remove the rest of the dishes from the table. She grabs a leftover cookie while eyeing a stack of DaySpring cards—leftover party favors. Suddenly I hear her gasp, "Mama! Can I have this card? The one with the door open on the front? I noticed it earlier today and I think it's meant just for me!"

I look over to see which one she's referring to and shrug. "Sure, baby! Consider it yours. What does it say, anyway?"

She looks up at me, her bright eyes dancing. She reads the front first and then the middle:

Even if it seems some doors are closing . . .

you haven't missed a thing.

God is going to open up the right one *just for you*.

Faith waves the card triumphantly in the air. "See?" she says, grinning a country mile wide. "I told you it was meant for me!" I smile past the lump in my throat. Past the memories of many difficult months and past all the ways I wished she didn't have to go through such a trial.

And then I arrive at the destination I wouldn't trade for anything: the one where Faith has learned that giving up gives her a new depth to her faith, a faith unimaginable several months earlier. She is stretching, all right. She is strengthening her faith muscles and gaining a flexible spirit. She is growing closer to her God and knows he sees her.

When seasons of intense change loom around us and shake us to our core, we remember God can't help but keep his promises. His character reflects it and his history proves it. With a more flexible spirit and a strengthened outlook, we see that the change sitting in front of us is not our stumbling block to contentment but rather one of the stepping-stones toward it.

So go ahead and give up. Give up and gain a flexible spirit.

While you're at it, let your trust in God boss around your feelings about change instead of the other way around.

Prayer

Dear Father in heaven, when we sit in change, thank you for giving us the freedom to straight up give up. Thank you for your everlasting love that marks my life with countless examples of your faithful care. And thank you for your unchanging loving-kindness that encourages me to keep a flexible spirit through change's middle seasons. When I start to believe this change may do me in, may I look at the life of Abraham and remember you don't send change alone: you send it with the promise of blessing. May I believe that this change is one way you open new doors meant just for me. In the hopeful name of Jesus, amen.

5

Accepting Limitations

War against stagnation. We are called to be pilgrims, not campers.

Dominic Done

I may be a person who has imperfectly learned to thrive *through* change, but I can't say I thrive *on* change. One itty-bitty preposition, one big ol' difference. Sure, if you told me you'd like to change my plans next month to include a European vacation, then I could thrive on that. Or if for some reason it suddenly became possible to Apparate, Harry Potter style, to any location in an instant—say, where my faraway family or friends live—I'd take that kind of magic change with easy excitement. I'd even take certain unmagical changes, like my children deciding they would like to keep their bedrooms somewhere close to cleanish. But as you read in the introduction and chapter 1, I don't necessarily go about looking for change on grand or garden variety levels. I don't get an adrenaline high from it. Sure, I like change that's my idea brought on my timetable, but I've lived most of my life okay with change showing up less often than it does for folks like my friend Tsh.

Tsh is a sweet writer friend I got to know first through her inspiring words at her blog, *The Art of Simple*, and later as a fellow writer for *(in)courage*, the blog of DaySpring. Tsh's life includes much travel, often to some of the most far-flung parts of the world. She and her family have hopscotched across the globe and lived everywhere from Turkey in the Middle East to Oregon in the United States and several places in between.

As I've read Tsh's writing through the years, I've come across this sentence in her words and stories more than once: "I thrive on change."

Well, that's one sentence yours truly has said *never*.

But I know God gives different people different personalities, interests, and bents. Some people enjoying change more than others is not so different from some enjoying the mountains more than beaches or chocolate more than vanilla. Still, I wonder if having the personality that thrives on change is helpful when it comes time to thrive through a change you didn't look for, like a change that found Tsh last winter.

On a bright, snowy day in central Oregon, Tsh and her family decided to choose from the list of ski resorts within a few hours of their home to enjoy some fresh air and fresh powder. They made their choice and headed out the door to their handpicked ski area. Things were going well on the slopes until Tsh, an experienced skier, got her ski caught in a clump of snow twenty feet down a black-level run. Down she went when mid-spin, her foot went one way while her knee went the other.

Hello, surgery and months of physical therapy. Good-bye, walking without crutches.

Not the kind of change any person would relish, right? Yes, but Tsh had wise words to say about the experience:

> I'm learning to burrow deep in to the God of my blessings, because my husband is amazing and doing the work of two parents while I sit and watch. I can read bedtime stories, fold the laundry, and review the week's spelling words. I can thankfully work, because writing requires a laptop and a chair, and I have access to both. And I still have half a lap for my two-year-old to shimmy up and snuggle in my arms, because he wants his mama despite that pesky leg brace. . . . "I believe that I shall look upon the goodness of the Lord in the land of the living" (Ps. 27:13).[1]

Tsh handled this change by keeping her eyes on what hadn't changed. But more than that, she looked at the limitations created by her changed circumstances and flipped them in her hand to see the goodness hiding underneath them. Her husband, Kyle, was there doing what he always does: helping in whatever way he can. She had more focused snuggle time with her babies. She had certain household distractions removed and was able to better concentrate on work.

Now, you may read this and say to me, "Yes, Kristen. This is true. But Tsh is wired to like change. So even if she didn't ask for a broken knee, isn't she better equipped to handle the change because her personality is bent toward liking it more? You don't know me and my circumstances, or my personality that's a limitation to being able to fully embrace change like that."

As one who has that personality limitation herself, I understand the question. But I also believe that every one of us must learn something about thriving through uninvited change. Even Tsh has mentioned experiencing seasons where she ached for a steady flow of sameness and struggled with accepting unwanted change. But the reason she *does* finally accept it is because she is able to find the blessings within it.

Every one of us must learn something about thriving through uninvited change.

There's nothing new under the sun, and each imperfect person comes with her own set of handicaps that adversely affect how she overcomes the challenges brought by a season of change. While some people seek change more than others, difficult change affects everyone, and everyone must learn to thrive through it, not just those of us who struggle with change on a broader level.

It's easy to forget that I'm far from the first person to have dealt with circumstances like these set in motion by change. Okay, I'll acknowledge that the girl over there faced a similar struggle, but she is doing fine because she's just tough. She's got more support. She's more laid-back. She hasn't been handed the same setbacks or limitations as I have, so therefore she has a head start in learning to thrive through her circumstances.

It may be harder for some to thrive, perhaps, but that doesn't mean it's not doable. It doesn't mean that God doesn't wholeheartedly desire this for you. And accepting that truth means accepting it's possible for you to thrive too.

So, fellow change-dislikers: How do we start removing the excuses we see as limitations preventing us from accepting change? In one hand we can hold on to Tsh's approach of being quick to flip change over to see the blessings underneath. And in the other we can look at those parts of our lives—like our limitations—and begin first to accept them and second to figure out how to thrive through them.

Who's the Boss?

Thinking about this topic of limitations takes me back a long (long, *long*) time to my eleventh-grade English class. I had an appreciation for literature and a knack for writing, so English came easily to me, and I usually managed to get an A. However, one semester of eleventh grade was different. I had one major limitation when it came to school, and that limitation smacked me on the backside that semester of English: I liked to talk. Before class. After class. *During class.* I could chat with my friends the whole livelong day and not think a thing about it.

That particular year, my English class had two of my BFFs in it, Cathy and Amy. It was the best. And the worst. Because even after Mrs. Cavener told the class to quiet down, I usually kept talking. Of course, I tried to be discreet about it—I would watch to make sure she wasn't looking before I leaned over to my left or turned around to say something to my gal pals. But either I wasn't as crafty at hiding my chatter as I thought or Mrs. Cavener had eagle eyes (or both). Either way, she knew I talked. And unlike most of my high school teachers, she whacked points off your grade for talking in class. So when she called me up at the end of the first quarter to tell me my grade, I was surprised when she said it was a B.

"What?!" I replied to her, hands perched on my hips. "But Mrs. Cavener, I've made As on most of my papers and tests."

She smiled up at me before tapping my name in her grade book. "Yes, Kristen, you absolutely did. But you get a B because you lost 8 whole percentage points for talking excessively in class. See here? You had a 95 percent before you lost your points for talking. You might want to work on that for the next quarter."

I was annoyed to say the least. My incredulous sixteen-year-old self thought, *Getting a B when I did A work for the class? Ridiculous! She's the one who keeps letting me sit by my friends! Can I help it if I'm chatty?* Of course, grown-up me grins at that sixteen-year-old and says, "Um, yes, you can, m'dear." When I whined about it to my parents, they told me the exact same thing. By holding me accountable for my own actions, Mrs. Cavener gave me serious incentive to learn how to zip my lips during class. I learned a valuable lesson about not letting my own limitation be an excuse for not thriving at my potential.

I could have taken another approach, however. Instead of resolving to change my behavior, what if I just shrugged my shoulders and thought, *Hey, I like to talk, I'm wired to talk, and I can't do much about that. It's just my personality?* Or what if my mom and dad made like helicopter parents and swooped down to Mrs. Cavener's class to tell her, "Listen, no one knows more than us that our girl likes to chat and it's impossible for her to stay quiet. Please just recognize this limitation in her and give her an A, okay?"

Not only would either of those scenarios have harmed me in the long run by enabling me, but each would have prevented me from becoming the boss of my limitation and therefore allowed it to stay the boss of me. Yes, it might have been a little more difficult for me to get an A in the class because of my propensity to talk, but that was no excuse for me not to try harder and be more respectful of the teacher in the process.

When it comes to accepting the change in our lives, I believe a lot of us view the challenge like I viewed my chattiness in English class. We see the change itself as a steely gray, concrete limitation to thriving, not something to work through or around. Not something to flip over and study as something God wants to use for us rather than against us.

Here's the exciting thing: we can actually thrive through change *because of* the limitations themselves, not just in spite of them. Becoming more mindful of how much I talked in English class couldn't help but make me more mindful of how much I talked in algebra, a subject that didn't come easily to me and I needed to pay better attention in. Overcoming that limitation also meant I learned to raise the bar on what I could expect from myself. It was a first step in me learning not to resent my limitations but rather to use them to my advantage.

Limitations as Invitations

Life's limitations are God's invitation to change our expectations. Limitations unfold his intention to travel a narrower path of possibilities.

At times I have crossed my arms and refused to believe this and allowed the limitations change brings to turn me bitter and disgruntled. I have complained till the cows came home and wished things were different. I have refused God's invitation to believe his promises and character, instead believing I knew better.

Embracing our limitations is one way we accept the unacceptable that change brings.

Life's limitations are God's invitation to change our expectations.

In her beautiful, whimsical book *The Nesting Place*, Myquillyn Smith wrote a chapter entitled "Lovely Limitations." Now, granted, Myquillyn's words are in reference to limitations as they pertain to decorating our homes with limited budget, space, and resources. But much of what she says about how we view limitations is applicable to our hearts and lives as well. It is also applicable to learning how to accept the circumstances of our current life season. Myquillyn writes,

> We all love to point out our buts. We all believe our buts are special, that no one else has a but like ours. Our buts hold us back. Our buts have become a wonderful excuse to put off, whine, and give up. And just like the kind of butts with skin on them, we sometimes assume that if we just had a different but, our lives would be easier. Instead of learning to appreciate and use our buts to get us where we are going, we see them as holding us back.[2]

In other words, we need to get to where *we like big buts and we cannot lie.*

Myquillyn further states,

> Lovely Limitations aren't bad. . . . When you have no limits, you put off making a decision because there are so many

options. I've gotten to the point of craving limits, because I know that some of my best projects have come out of what I *didn't* have.[3]

Some of our most thriving days spring from accepting what circumstances have changed. For my daughter Faith, her neck injury put a holy stop on gymnastics, a definitive *This is not for you, precious daughter* from her heavenly Father. While she misses the sport, there is an undeniable freedom attached to the realization that some things aren't possible. It crosses some activities off the list and makes the choices simpler.

The removal of gymnastics from Faith's life gave her the option to explore uncharted waters: namely, competitive swimming. She discovered she loved the sport and actually begs to go to practice every day. Quite honestly, her talent in swimming far outshines her talent in gymnastics. But if gymnastics had never been removed from the table for her, I'm not sure she would have looked at the other options long enough to discover this.

Limitations are borders, boundaries that hem us in and keep us on the path God has prepared for us. Consider these words:

> I quit focusing on the handicap and began appreciating the gift. It was a case of Christ's strength moving in my weakness. Now I take limitations in stride, and with good cheer, these limitations that cut me down to size—abuse, accidents, opposition, bad breaks. I just let Christ take over! And so the weaker I get, the stronger I become. (2 Cor. 12:9–10 The Message)

In one form, limitations are boundaries. But in another, limitations are wide-open fields where I acknowledge my own weakness and accept I need Jesus to go the distance where I cannot. A limitation is a grace space for me to lie down in and soak up God's presence. It is a garden spot for me to reflect on God's believability.

When we spend all our energy wishing things were different, we have no strength to revel in the glory of the blessings right in front of us. Our limitations work for us, not against us. They also test us to see just how genuine our faith is.

Limitations as Waiting Tests

When limitations show up in the middle places, it's especially difficult to hold on to belief.

My husband and I both thought this in the months after we hoped to start a family. We assumed it would be as simple as it was for so many of our family and friends around us. We wanted to change our little family from two to three, but in the following months we learned that wanting a change wouldn't make it happen.

I wish I could tell you I took the waiting gracefully, that I sank into faith and patience and allowed each to be there for me. I didn't. Not getting pregnant seemed like an insurmountable limitation to me living well, and I spent a lot of time crying and crossing my arms to God. I looked at the ripe bellies of friends and family and begged God to open what was closed. When a friend or family member mentioned they were expecting, I did and said all the right things to their face but then crawled into bed and pulled up the covers. I let my limitation prevent me from being truly happy for our loved ones growing little ones.

In hindsight, I see the time I spent waiting to become pregnant for what it was: a test. And it was a test I straight up flunked. Of course, the inability to get pregnant was not the test. Oh no. The test was in how I spent that time waiting to become pregnant. And in short, I did not wait well. I believed my inability to carry a child was a giant, roadblock-sized limitation to my own ability to thrive. As discussed in chapter 3, it's a fine thing to mourn and be sad. But when I consistently wallow in tears rather than truth, I'm not doing myself any favors.

Contrast my behavior to that of my friend Jen.

Like me, Jen struggled to get pregnant. But unlike me, Jen's example of peace amidst the limitations that changed her plans was palpable. We met while living across the street from one another on a military base, and she was the kind of person I couldn't wait to become fast friends with: thoughtful, funny, and warm. My twin sons were two years old when we met, and she and her husband didn't mind babysitting them from time to time. She was an encourager in the realest sense (still is), and she didn't mind telling me if I had a great hair day or if she liked how I handled a particular parenting situation. Jen was the first person to invite me over for a Bible study featuring a book written by a dynamic, blonde-haired wonder named Beth Moore.

I watched and listened as Jen asked many of the same questions as I did in her desire to become pregnant. I also watched and listened as Jen came up with completely different answers from my own.

One early morning as the sun just began to split open the dark skies, Jen and I met in her driveway for our regular walk around the neighborhood. As we took off down Juniper Court, I asked her how she was feeling about things on the baby front. She looked at me before looking straight ahead, and I'll never forget her words. "You know, Kristen, some days are hard. Really hard. I want something so much, yet I know very well God may not give it to me. And as much as I pray his will is for John and me to be parents, there is a peace that comes with knowing his will for us will be what's best for us, regardless of the outcomes."

The grace in which she handled not receiving what she desperately wanted would have made the Duchess of Cambridge look clumsy. Her voice trembled, but there was a quiet strength in it too. It held both proof that she felt her struggle and also felt assured of God's provision, even if the provision looked different from what she wished.

The very struggle that could have made her question God propelled her faith in him forward. While I saw my inability to get pregnant as a limitation to thriving, Jen saw it as an invitation to draw closer to Christ. And in that, she thrived in spite of her circumstances. Does that mean she didn't have her own times of tears and wishing things were different? No. But it does mean she knew how to wallow in God's truth more than her tears.

I remember shaking my head at her words, wishing I could have grasped that kind of grace—and accepted that kind of faith—when my husband and I were dealing with infertility. Jen's response was one of those faith-defining moments for me, one that moved me miles more than her introduction to Beth Moore's Bible studies. The way she bravely spoke through her heartache showed me what it looked like to live knowing God's promises were totally and completely true. Jen's actions took "I should" words from flat pages in my mind and moved them to "I can" living actions of my heart. She taught me how to see a limitation as a test revealing how well I wait—and how to pass it.

Joseph's Story: Big Limitations and Bigger Faith

When I pick back up on Joseph's story in Genesis, I see another example of someone who passed his own waiting test and did not see change as a limitation to thriving.

As the servant in charge of everything Potiphar owned, Joseph spent much time in the presence of Potiphar's family. He lived in Potiphar's home, and Genesis 39 says that because Joseph did such a fantastic job taking care of everything belonging to Potiphar, "he did not concern himself with anything except the food he ate" (v. 6). As Joseph moved about his daily duties, Mrs. Potiphar, feeling too ignored or too entitled, moved in on the good lookin', well-built servant.

I picture Mrs. Potiphar sauntering up to Joseph after double-checking that her husband is out of earshot. In a breathy tone like Marilyn Monroe, she says to him, "Come to bed with me!" (Gen. 39:7). She propositions him not just once but time after time.

What does Scripture say Joseph did? He refused. Not just once but time after time.

It couldn't have been easy to refuse her. His job was demanding and stressful. Joseph was handed an entire set of limitations as deep as the well he'd been thrown in, and he could have thought he deserved to cut loose and have a little fun with the lady of the house. Given Potiphar's wealth and connections, odds are good his wife had the face of a Hollywood celebrity and the body of a Victoria Secret model. Joseph was a man with healthy desires, and he could have felt entitled to exercise them.

But Joseph gave her a firm and unequivocal no, saying, "My master withheld nothing from me except you, because you are his wife. How then could I do such a wicked thing and sin against God?" (Gen. 39:9).

Joseph had more on his mind than dishonoring his master. He didn't want to sin against God, either. Sometimes when a test comes, we can't use our limitations as permission slips to get out of it. During those times, we need to cling to what we know is right, even if that answer goes against what our flesh wants.

When Joseph made that choice, he probably thought the test was over and thanked God for giving him the wisdom to pass. But Mrs. Potiphar wouldn't take rejection sitting down. She proceeded to tell her husband another version of the story, saying Joseph tried to crawl in bed with her until she screamed for help. Potiphar believed her and had Joseph thrown in prison.

So much for taking the high road. The high road took Joseph down to the lowest part of the household: the dungeon. The hits just kept coming for him, and I wonder if Joseph's mood ever fell as far as his fall from the top. Perhaps so, but instead of complaining, Joseph used the opportunity to make an impression.

> But while Joseph was there in the prison, the LORD was with him; he showed him kindness and granted him favor in the eyes of the prison warden. So the warden put Joseph in charge of all those held in the prison, and he was made responsible for all that was done there. (Gen. 39:20–22)

Whatever the crummy circumstances, Joseph put his best foot forward, kept God at the forefront of his mind, and simply did the best he could at any given moment. In his doing so, a limitation turned itself into a favorable impression because Joseph refused to believe anything other than that God was still watching over his life. In that dark, damp prison, Joseph clung to the warmth of God's promise that against all odds, his circumstances would be redeemed and God still had good things planned for him.

Later we will read about how Joseph not only made a good impression on the prison warden but also made a good impression on Pharaoh. After enduring two more years in prison, he would oversee much more than just the prison. Joseph was asked to interpret a dream for Pharaoh, and because God blessed him with clear explanations, Pharaoh was impressed. He was so impressed, he put Joseph in charge of his palace and said, "Only with respect to the throne will I be greater than you" (Gen. 41:40).

From the dungeon's destitution to Pharaoh's VIP. How many folks have traveled such a distance in a day?

Max Lucado wrote the following in regard to Joseph's story:

> God is fully engaged. He sees the needs of tomorrow and, accordingly, uses your circumstances to create the test of today. . . . Trust his training. You'll get through this. If God can make a prince out of a prisoner, don't you think he can make something good out of your mess?[4]

When undesirable change brings limitations in the form of waiting our way, do we believe God still has our best in mind? Or do we believe he's forgotten us somewhere along the way? Or maybe we *know* God wants what is best for us, but we *live* like we believe he's forgotten us. I want to trust his training and believe that he is gathering up all the threads of my messy life and making something beautiful with it.

Do I get an A on every faith test? Hardly. Sometimes I pass with a little ease; sometimes I pass by the skin of my teeth. Sometimes I flat-out fail and need a do-over. But when change comes, my heart is learning to not see it as a limitation to thriving. My heart is learning to turn it over and see it *as a means to thrive*. My heart is learning to believe that change always comes with God's promise of blessings.

The Wonder in Waiting

My baby girl, only weeks old, lies sleeping in the blue-and-white checked stroller. Her brothers, both lively and curious three-year-olds, pedal their tricycles slowly down Juniper Court as we all trek toward the base indoor pool for swim lessons. By the time we round the corner onto Pennsylvania Street, I'm already fussing at James and Ethan to keep moving. I silently scold myself for not having the forethought to leave for the swim lessons sooner.

James halts pedaling altogether and calls ahead to me, "Mama! Did you *see* dis bug ovuh here? He's duh biggest bug I've evuh seen!" I turn around to see him leaning low over his silver trike toward a black speck on the ground.

I answer quickly, "Yes, I did see that big bug. C'mon, James, we need to move on."

He reluctantly presses onward. Ten seconds later, I hear Ethan screech to a halt on his trike. I turn around again to find something holding his fascination.

I can't hold in my annoyance, and exasperation leaks from all corners of my voice: "Ethan! We *reeeaally* need to keep going. Hurry up, baby!"

He reaches down and picks up something next to his brown strapped sandals.

"Just a minute, Mama! I just *have* to get dis wock. Just wait 'til you see all de coluhs on it!"

I sigh and stroll backward a bit to look at the colorful rock. Its colors glint and sparkle in the desert sunshine, and I tell him it is beautiful. He shoves it in his pocket and then starts moving again.

Like so many children, my toddlers moved slowly when I needed them to move quickly and moved quickly when I'd rather they slow down. It wouldn't be until much later when I tossed those memories from one corner of my mind to the other that I would understand how much better little James and Ethan understood the art of waiting: little ones know that waiting leaves room for the wonder.

For much of my life, I equated waiting time with wasted time. I saw waiting as the lazy roommate on the sofa, the one who drops more potato chip crumbs between the cushions than a preschooler and never seems to have money for rent. I looked at her with squinty eyes while aching to scream the words, "Hey, would you get off your backside and move to help out a little around here?"

On that morning with my littles, I saw the bug and the rock as limitations to getting to swim lessons on time. But James and Ethan saw them as a means to wonder. The wait time wasn't a bother because it gave them the opportunity to pause, admire, and savor. They taught me (in addition to the importance of scheduling real time for the wonder by leaving for all places earlier) that the wait time isn't dead time; it's time spent awake and alive to all God wants to show and give us. And in that, children always prove what Arthur Gordon says: "Pausers are not time-wasters; they are time-*users*."[5]

When I am asked to do the hard waiting during my season of change, I need to ask myself, "Kristen, are you wasting this time or using it?" Am I letting the perceived limitation of time be my boss or am I going to show it who's boss by using it? God means to use all time for me, not against me. When the odds look tall against me and my limitations seem especially foreboding, God is not idle. I don't need to resent the wait. I need to hold on to the belief that what I see around me may look slow to move, but in it God moves in perfect time. I want to remember the waiting time as a time to wonder how God is going to move on my behalf.

Wait time isn't dead time; it's time spent awake and alive to all God wants to show and give us.

I want to remember Abraham, who did not keep his eyes on his limitation in the form of advanced age and believed God would make him the father of nations anyway.

I want to remember Tsh, who believes there are blessings found inside limitations.

I want to remember Jen, whose life displays vibrant colors of God's promises, limitations and all.

I want to remember Joseph, who used time well by simply honoring God in the midst of the most unpleasant circumstances.

Sister-friend, the Lord is moving for you right this second, weaving the good and bad circumstances of your life into hope-filled beauty. He doesn't take time off from you or need a break from your circumstances. You are always in the forefront of his thoughts, and he is always working toward what's best for you.

After all, his love for you—and his ways of caring for you—are limitless.

Prayer

Dear Father in heaven, thank you that no limitation could ever keep me separated from you. As I contemplate all the places I have allowed my real or imagined limitations to boss me around, please show me the ways you want me to thrive not in spite of them but maybe even because of them. Show me that as I wait out seasons of change, the wait itself is not a limitation but an invitation to seek the wonder of how you work on my behalf. May I see my limitations as your invitation to unfold your intentions. And as I move about among my family and friends, may I be a light that reflects the wonder of your love. In the mighty name of Jesus, amen.

6

Light in a Windowless Room

> When a train goes through a tunnel and it gets dark, you don't throw away the ticket and jump off. You sit still and trust the engineer.
>
> Corrie ten Boom

I t is true that the bleakest of limitations in our circumstances can't dampen the light gratitude brings.

I kissed Faith on the forehead as she drifted off to sleep, wishing like mad we were in her bright purple painted bedroom rather than this sterile green operating room. If only she were drifting off to sleep before a date with friends instead of drifting off to sleep before a date with a surgeon who would operate on her spine. I continued to whisper, *"Jesus is here, Jesus is here,"* long after she closed her eyes.

I said it for me as much as for her.

I carefully got off her gurney and said a quick prayer of thanks that the children's hospital in our town let me ride on it with Faith right through the swinging metal double doors to the OR. A caring nurse named Mary hugged me in the kindest, warmest way and whispered reassuring words as she patted my back. (I never met a Mary I didn't like.) I responded by sobbing, because the best way to get shaky Kristen teetering on the edge of an emotional breakdown to lose it is to hug me.

I walked out through the oversized swinging doors into the steady, already open arms of David. We walked in a half hug to the waiting room of the hospital.

As David held the door open for me, I walked in and quickly scanned the waiting room. My knee-high brown boots stopped dead in their tracks. My eyes darted around the room again, and I stood there slack-jawed while shaking my head back and forth.

David, noticing my frozen posture and expression, came up next to me. "What's wrong?" he asked, following my eyes around to the room.

My arm moved to find his and grabbed it.

"What's wrong?" I repeated, annoyed that he was missing the obvious. "It's . . . it's this *room*, David!" I stammered, whirling in a circle and pointing. "Just look! There are *no windows* in this room!"

His eyes swept the room again. Sensing what was coming, he began rubbing my back in short, quick pats while whispering quietly but quickly, "No, but I think—"

I wheeled around to meet his eyes.

"What were they *thinking* to make a hospital waiting room without windows? Who could have designed such a thing? How are families supposed to wait out their babies' surgeries in a room without any way to see outside?" My hands flew up and down, up and down. "How is one supposed to feel hopeful in this . . . this *tomb*?"

David pulled me in close, mind going a mile a minute trying to figure out the quickest way to calm me down. I leaned against him, ignoring the overt stares of others. I cried so hard my breathing turned shallow, and David said, "Baby, it's okay, *it's okay*. Why don't we go to the cafeteria and wait for a bit? Maybe it has windows. The doctor won't call here with a progress report for some time, so we don't have to wait here right now."

I nodded up and down and let him usher me out of the room and toward the cafeteria. I must have been holding my breath, because when we arrived at the cafeteria and I saw an outside view, I exhaled. I grabbed myself a cup of tea and took a couple disinterested drinks while staring outside through the tall windows. Bright December sunlight drenched everything, and I put my hand on the glass to steep in a bit of it, to let it warm me on the inside.

Gratitude provides a window to a windowless room.

Before long, we walked back to the dark waiting room to wait for a progress report from the OR. After going inside and finding two chairs in a corner, I set my mostly full teacup down and lowered my head into my hands. Still muttering about poor building plans and the injustice of a windowless waiting room, I heard the Lord say to me straight out, *"Gratitude provides a window to a windowless room."*

I guess he heard me complaining.

He stopped my downward spiral with plain truth: gratitude is the way of hope, especially during seasons of difficult change. When change wipes all the natural light from the rooms of my heart, being thankful is the way to usher it back in. Being thankful helps me creak open bolted shutters and knock holes in thick walls.

Leaning against David's shoulder, I said quietly:

Thank you God, for an excellent pediatric neurosurgeon in our town.

Thank you for a husband not deployed and home to do this with me.

Thank you for the Petersens watching our other children.

Thank you for countless family and friends who are holding us all in prayer.

Thank you for this room where your presence beams, windows or not.

Corrie's Story: Gratitude before the Miracle

Corrie ten Boom is one of my favorite heroines of faith, and her book *The Hiding Place* details her life's drastic change after the Nazi invasion and occupation of her home country, the Netherlands. During that long, dark period, her family's participation in the Dutch Underground helped save many Jews from the Nazi Holocaust. However, a Dutch informant reported the ten Boom family to the Nazis for their work, and they were all arrested. Later, Corrie, along with her sister Betsie, was taken to Ravensbrück concentration camp deep inside the dark forests of Germany.

After surviving horrendous events in Ravensbrück's temporary dorms—grueling marches, standing for hours at parade attention, and humiliating medical inspections—Corrie and Betsie were eventually shown their permanent dormitories.

Once inside, their senses immediately told them the plumbing was backed up and the bedding was rancid. Fighting nausea, Corrie climbed to her own pallet in the sleeping quarters and suddenly felt a pinch on her leg. Realizing their straw mattresses were infested with fleas, she cried out to her sister, totally lost as to how they could live in such a place. Betsie immediately pointed her to the Bible passage they had read earlier in the week:

> Pray continually, give thanks in all circumstances; for this is God's will for you in Christ Jesus. (1 Thess. 5:17–18)

Betsie urged Corrie to be thankful for everything, even the fleas. Corrie thought thanking God for the fleas was just too much, and she told her sister there was no way even God could make her thankful for a flea. Betsie continued to point her toward Scripture, reminding her the passage said to be thankful in all circumstances, not just the pleasant ones. So both sisters sat inside that flea-infested room thanking God for each miserable one.[1]

As the story continued, Corrie discovered exactly why she should be thankful for the fleas. Corrie, Betsie, and the other residents of that dormitory never understood why they were given so much freedom in their large room. They openly held prayer services, sang hymns, and walked around sharing the gospel with anyone and everyone inside. And they did it all without being discovered. As it turns out, the supervisors and guards at Ravensbrück knew that dormitory was infested with fleas, so none of them wanted anything to do with it. Indeed, the biting fleas turned into a saving grace.

I can't help but wonder: When I sit in change, what are the dark things that bite? What are the fleas in the dark places that seem impossible to be grateful for? The biting things usually look more cursed than blessed, don't they? The biting remarks from the older relative about your weight. The biting comments from the man in the checkout line about your parenting. The biting review from the colleague at work who undervalues your contributions. The situations and actions that snap hard and sting much. You feel the *bite, bite, bite* of their words and actions, and no matter how often you scratch, you cannot rid yourself of their imprint. How are you supposed to be thankful for any of that? If you're like me, it's way easier and more satisfying in the short term to just sit and massage your wounds.

But just maybe by offering up your gratitude *in all* things, you are also showing how you trust God *to use all* things too. It's one way you put feet and wings to your belief, to let proof of Christ's love into your heart. It may feel contrary to what you want to do, but in the long term, that will be the medicine that heals.

God asks us to show him gratitude in the dark because he knows that's how we find him in the dark. When we look around our

Maybe by offering up your gratitude in all things, you are also showing how you trust God to use all things too.

windowless rooms and aren't sure what to do, we say what we're thankful for out loud because that forces light through the densest walls. Gratitude again brings the sun and fresh air to the windowless times in our soul and reminds us of what we have. The focus on what is missing blurs, and the focus on what is present sharpens.

The focus on Who is present sharpens.

While those inside Corrie and Betsie's barracks still experienced unimaginable suffering, they also experienced a growth in camaraderie and friendship that set them apart from residents in other barracks. Without the watchful eyes of the camp guards, Corrie and Betsie were able to share the love of Jesus, and because of it, Jesus grew in the hearts of the women there. He was light in windowless barracks.

Some of my favorite words written on gratitude are by Ann Voskamp. She writes:

> "*On the night he was betrayed,* the Lord Jesus took some bread and *gave thanks to God for it.*" . . . Jesus, on the night before the driving hammer and iron piercing through ligament and sinew, receives what God offers as grace (*charis*), the germ of his thanksgiving (*eucharistia*)? Oh. Facing the abandonment of God Himself (does it get any worse that this?), Jesus offers thanksgiving for even that which will break him and crush him and wound him and yield a bounty of joy (*chara*). The mystery always contains more mysteries.[2]

It is the mystery we enter into by choosing gratitude:

> Jesus took the bread and gave thanks . . . and then the miracle of Jesus enduring the cross for the joy set before Him. . . . *Eucharisteo*—thanksgiving—*always precedes the miracle.*[3]

We enter into the miracle when we first give thanks.

Do you believe you need a miracle to accept your change? Something to *do* to make the situation better right here and now?

Then perhaps you and I can turn our faces toward the light of thankfulness. When Corrie and Betsie did, they saw miserable fleas transform to miraculous freedoms. But they were *first* thankful and *second* received the miracle: church in the middle of a concentration camp.

Thanksgiving always precedes the miracle.

Gratitude Is God-timistic

My daughter, Faith, never shies from hard questions, and one comes up while she is splayed out on my bed with me. Her brother Ethan sits perched on the end. After talking about the same verse Betsie directed Corrie to in 1 Thessalonians, the one that instructs us to be thankful in all circumstances, Faith looks up at me. With a deep furrow over her smoky blue eyes, she says, "But Mama, I don't know *how* to be thankful in all circumstances. Does that mean I'm supposed to be thankful I broke my neck?"

I look at her and brush her honey-colored hair away from her face. I think about my daddy who has multiple sclerosis. About the military wife attending her husband's funeral. About all the Corrie ten Booms who suffered evil's most horrific forms. Isn't it asking too much to be thankful for the hard realities brought on by drastic change?

I meet her eyes before snuggling up next to her on the bed.

"Well, Faith, it does say to give thanks in *all* circumstances, so I think that includes circumstances of broken bones. But I know it's hard to say, 'God, thank you for allowing my neck to be broken.' Perhaps instead you could say, 'God, thank you for not letting my broken neck go to waste.' You can be thankful that your story doesn't end in something broken but instead in something healed. You can be thankful for what God worked through that situation and that your broken neck brought about many good things, including a new love for swimming and a deeper awareness of how close Jesus is to you. This is how you give thanks in all circumstances: you believe that God's goodness is in all circumstances, and you show you believe by telling God *thank you*."

She is quiet, deep in thought. Then she says with a little exhale, "Oh, that makes sense."

Could it be that gratitude brings a measure of sense to the senseless?

Ethan looks up and says, "So it's not about having an optimistic attitude when it comes to gratitude. It's about having a *God-timistic* one."

I tilt my head toward him and one corner of my mouth turns up in a smile. "Well, I never thought about it like that, but you're right. It's about remembering how God sheds light on everything, that darkness is as light to him, and no matter how the dark pierces, God's goodness pierces deeper and higher."

Later I look up the original meaning of the word *optimism* and see it is derived from the Latin *optimum*, meaning "the greatest good."[4] Isn't God always going about working to bring the greatest good to our lives? Being God-timistic is knowing that God only allows pain if the gain is to be greater.

God uses what is broken on the outside to heal what is broken on the inside. That is the work being done in the dark, the work we cannot see. He is the Lord who heals (see Exod. 15:26). He is the Lord who restores and wants us to be whole—really, genuinely, totally whole. And while we may sit in the dark outside and need a light to shine, we also may sit in the dark inside and need a light to shine in. When we train our eyes to look for ways to be thankful, we are trusting

God to do both. Being God-timistic is being aware that God is always working for our gain.

One God-timistic person who lived this was Moses. He wanted to experience closeness with God, and his desires were met on an unimaginable scale. He spent an extraordinary amount of time with God on Mount Sinai and wanted still more. But then again, that's the nature of how God works. The more time you spend with him, the more you want to spend time with him.

In Exodus 33, Moses makes what sounds like a mighty bold request when he tells God, "Show me your glory" (v. 18). But what Moses really wants is to experience God in all possible ways. He wants to be as close to God as possible.[5] God grants Moses his request with one caveat. Knowing a straight-on view of his glory would be too much for Moses to take in, God tells Moses he may see his glory from behind. To protect him, God places Moses in the crevice of a rock and covers him with his hand while passing by.

I am not unfamiliar with the idea that says to know God's glory, we are sometimes asked to sit in tight places. But as I read those verses from Exodus, what I uncover is this: When change puts me in tight places, is it especially dark because his hand covers and protects me too? Can I believe—really believe—it is dark because of mercy and protection rather than abandonment?

> The Lord granted that which would abundantly satisfy. God's goodness is his glory; and he will have us to know him by the glory of his mercy, more than by the glory of his majesty. Upon the rock there was a fit place for Moses to view the goodness and glory of God.[6]

As we maneuver change from our own tight places, we could stop for a moment and see that tight place as a fit place to still find the goodness and glory of God.

When I feel the heartbreak over all the ways multiple sclerosis cripples my daddy, I see a fit place for God's goodness in the way my family and friends care for him.

When the woman going through chemo feels the squeeze of fragile life, she sees a fit place for God's goodness in others walking the journey with her.

When the mother feels the stab of ugly words spoken from her growing child, she sees a fit place for God's goodness in the opportunity to lift him up in prayer.

We all have the opportunity to turn our tight places into prayer spaces. When change shoves us to our knees in dark places, we are in the perfect posture for lifting up our souls to heaven. We are not left alone. The hand of God hovers over us, protecting us always.

Wandering in the Dark

The Israelites were happy to be freed from Pharaoh for all of ten seconds before the complaining began. Not long after the waters of the Red Sea stitched back together, the *if onlys* spilled into the desert air.

If only we had the food we had in Egypt!

If only we had more water!

If only we had a god to go before us!

Sometimes we are no better. We think change is good until we've had just enough of it to decide that the grass on the first hill was lusher and greener after all. Never mind how we are several steps closer to freedom. Never mind the miracles that walk each step with us. Change it back to the way it was before!

God is close to us amidst difficult change, providing for us, nurturing our physical, spiritual, and mental needs. But it can be hard to see it when we are surrounded by hardship and pain.

A portion of Nehemiah lists all the ways God's compassion reigned during the Israelites' years of wandering:

His presence stayed with them by day in a pillar of cloud and by night in a pillar of fire.

His Holy Spirit instructed them.

He provided food and water.

And then Nehemiah gets blessedly specific: "For forty years you sustained them in the desert; they lacked nothing, their clothes did not wear out nor did their feet become swollen" (Neh. 9:21).

The Israelites may have been meandering through a parched desert, but they were not abandoned. They weren't comfortable, but they were comforted. From pillars in the sky to intact threads of clothing, God's powerful presence showed itself in grand and humble ways. However, the Israelites wandered aimlessly because time and again, they focused on what they didn't have rather than on what they did.

Gratitude keeps us from wandering in the dark. It is a compass that always reverts us back to true North, the Bright Morning Star. It is the way we say to God, "I believe that you are always out for my greatest good because I see you moving in my life right here, right now."

I forget this. I go through a season of change, and I heavily spice it with complaints and starve it of gratitude. I make like a toddler who balks every time she doesn't get what she wants *right this second*. One day, in the middle of my temper tantrum, the Lord gently but firmly spoke these exact words right into my spirit: "Kristen, if you will not be thankful for a few things, why should I give you many things?"

Why indeed. Gratitude isn't something we remember every once in a while during the good times. It's something we remember every day, no matter the season. It is what Dietrich Bonhoeffer spoke of when he wrote,

> *Gratitude keeps us from wandering in the dark*

> Only he who gives thanks for the little things receives the big things. We prevent God from giving us the great spiritual gifts he has in store for us, because we do not give thanks for daily gifts. . . . We pray for the big things and forget to give thanks for the ordinary, small (and yet really not small) gifts.[7]

I imagine myself putting a cork in the channel of blessings because I would rather search the flat horizons for bigger things than look at what sits in the curve of my hands.

When change comes like a rowdy child knocking what we hold dear off the table, we can still be thankful for the table. We can still be thankful that like the table, hope stands.

Sherri's Story: Finding a Window of Hope

Sherri was a successful professional in the corporate world when she fell in love with and married a handsome fellow named Daniel. Not long after relocating to a new town, Sherri learned she was pregnant with their first child. Daniel's work required him to travel frequently, so Sherri knew she'd be doing much of the preparation for the new baby solo. Occasionally this stressed and frustrated Sherri, especially since they lived several hours from her family and she didn't have a good support system in their new town. But Sherri took it one day at a time, choosing to focus on the realities of what needed to get done more than on how she longed for more help.

Nine months later, Sherri gave birth to a healthy, beautiful baby girl. Her husband still traveled quite a lot, but when he was home they enjoyed their time together and settled into new family routines. Sherri felt quite content in her small family's life.

Not long after the birth of their first daughter, Sherri discovered she was pregnant again. Tagging along with that news was the announcement that her husband had been offered a promotion that would relocate them to the same town where her family lived. Sherri was thrilled. Adding a second baby to their family as well as moving back home—she was getting everything she had ever hoped and dreamed.

But then her celebration was cut short at the doctor's office by the news that her baby had no heartbeat—and probably had not had one for at least two weeks. Since a natural miscarriage risked complications so late after nonviability of pregnancy, Sherri had a D&C procedure. Guilt over that procedure hung around her, and it took time for her to shake off the cloak of empty sadness. Hugging her precious little girl, Sherri did her best to dwell less on her sorrows than her blessings.

Life went on, and Sherri worked hard to move right along with it. They relocated and bought a gorgeous home down the street and around the corner from her parents. And then, three short months after moving in, Daniel, who was in the National Guard, left for an overseas deployment. The time spent caring for her daughter alone during the deployment was hard, but Sherri did what she always did: shifted to her automatic posture of "just keep moving" and kept in time with the flow.

Five months later, the deployment ended and Sherri welcomed Daniel home. Daniel went back to his usual schedule in his civilian job, which meant catching up at work and traveling. When her husband was home, Sherri felt Daniel was distant, but they kept trucking along on the familiar roads of family routines. Not much later, Sherri found out she was pregnant again and quickly concluded the pregnancy was why things felt "different."

In late summer, Sherri and Daniel's second daughter turned them from a family of three into a family of four. Sherri and Daniel adjusted once again and enjoyed deepening bonds with their precious daughters. With two young children, Sherri would still get frustrated with her husband's intense traveling. But when she would look at her girls' sweet faces and remember how blessed she was to stay at home with them, she stifled her complaints. She would keep on keepin' on.

Then came the news of Daniel's second deployment with the National Guard.

With this deployment, Sherri's fears came out of the corners bigger and meaner. Not only would her husband be in a centralized combat zone, but she would be caring for a three-year-old and a three-month-old on her own—and for a longer stretch of time. Scenarios of a husband injured overseas or a break-in on the homefront filled her thoughts and dreams.

The deployment came and brought with it sick children, hospital visits, and more sleepless nights. But Sherri continued to get up each day and just put one foot in front of the other, leaning into Jesus while relying on family and friends for help.

Upon Daniel's return home, he got back to business in civilian life and quickly readjusted to his job. But at home, things did not settle nearly so smoothly. The strain in their relationship filled their walls and hearts and turned them into strangers. Sherri wanted to believe it was due to the time and distance apart, but in the quiet of night, she worried it was something more.

Then, on a cold winter evening, her husband gave the cold and crushing news: he had been unfaithful.

Despite the tremendous pain and betrayal she felt, Sherri fervently wanted the marriage to survive. She vowed to do everything in her power to help the relationship and make this happen. She prayed constantly that she would understand the root cause of their problems, and she begged God to show her what she could do differently. Sherri clung to the fact that if she could just work to fix what was wrong, the relationship would repair itself. After all, she loved Daniel deeply and believed an intact marriage was best for their girls.

In the meantime, she spent her nights tossing and turning through tears and her days making sure their daughters were as unaffected as possible. Although some days were okay, most were strained. Sherri constantly dealt with a double-sided reality: her husband's apologetic words filled with regret and his actions that spoke a very different story.

When Daniel was once again called up for a deployment, Sherri was almost relieved. While the thought of him in a war zone scared her, she believed this would be a good opportunity for them both to clear their heads and think about their marriage. With a little time and perspective, surely they would both see the situation more clearly and be able to pinpoint and fix their problems.

Instead, a few days before the deployment departure date, the severest change to date literally crashed down on Sherri's doorstep: she was served with "dissolution of marriage" papers. Her world rocked and tipped right over, dragging her hopes and dreams for her ideal family life with it. How could her husband *choose* to leave like this? So many feelings invaded her thoughts—betrayal, hurt, and anger in the top three. The tornado of emotions only stopped when questions bullied their way in. *Where will we live? How will I work and manage child care? What will people think of me? How will my church react? Will I be loved again?*

Many of the practical, logistical questions were answered along the way, but many others lingered like swarming mosquitos. A stronger tidal wave of emotions swirled around her, including a vivid sadness and defeated spirit. Guilt stabbed her—guilt over failing God and her girls because she couldn't keep her marriage together.

The growing anger she felt at her ex-husband filled in the cracks of her emotional state and ate at her ability to move forward. Sherri knew she had to relinquish that anger. She knew stewing on the actions of her ex-husband kept her focus on him rather than on getting herself to a healthy place.

So one evening after she put the girls to bed, Sherri began journaling a gratitude list. Within a week of beginning that project, she saw all the amazing ways God had prepared her for this situation. On her journal pages laid plain proof that before she knew what was to come, God did and equipped her in more ways than she realized.

Because of Daniel's extensive traveling, she was already accustomed to solo parenting.

She knew how to manage mothering and the household efficiently.

She lived in the same town as her family, so she had a good support system nearby.

She had met amazing friends and connected to a good church home.

Her relationship with the Lord deepened prior to the revealing of the affair, and so she had his presence to lean on and his promises to rely on.

Sherri continued to write out her thankfulness. And when all her good notions of the perfect family life fell apart, her journaling reminded her that Christ still moves through his perfect love for her to complete his good plans for her. With each new gratitude, the window of her heart would open a bit more. With each new gratitude, her focus sharpened on Christ.

For a long while, Sherri told only those very close to her about the divorce, while by and large she hid behind shame and embarrassment. She didn't know how to just stand up in church or at preschool and announce, "Hey everyone! By the way, I'm now divorced." In hindsight, she wishes she had been more forthcoming earlier on. When she finally began to be more open about what was happening in her life to a wider circle of people, the outpouring of love and support from her friends and church members blew her away. She realized then that instead of silently suffering, she could have been surrounded by the outpouring of soul-filling encouragement much earlier.

While time and a deeper depending on Jesus gradually pulled back the curtains on her joy and hope, a small part of her held on to anger and resentment. She knew she was called to forgive Daniel just as Jesus forgives her. But the feelings just weren't there. Sherri wanted to rid her heart of this once and for all, so she prayed and asked the Lord to help her forgive, *really fully* forgive Daniel.

The following Sunday morning at church, she felt especially compelled to release the anger. She wanted to fully embrace the biggest change thus far: to be free of the past and move forward into the future. She wanted to loosen the chains so she could thrive in all the ways God intended. It was a communion Sunday, and as Sherri knelt at the altar, she listened to her pastor speak timeless words of grace and forgiveness. She took the bread, savoring the promises of the Lord with it too. *"The Lord Jesus, on the night he was betrayed, took bread, and when he had given thanks, he broke it and said, 'This is my body, which is for you; do this in remembrance of me.'"* As she ate the bread, Sherri felt just how real Jesus's presence was with her. She knew Jesus remembers her just as assuredly as she was remembering him at the communion table. Sherri prayed right there that the Lord would take all her anger. As she sat deep in conversation with God, she missed the wine offering. She missed the parting words of her pastor. She only realized communion was over because she heard the rustling of those around her as they stood to leave.

Sherri stood too, feeling renewed and whole again. She thanked God for doing what she could not do on her own. And she knew a thing or two about doing things on her own. She could write a book on how to push through on her own strength. Pick yourself up by your bootstraps? Heck, Sherri knew how to pick herself up with much less. But she couldn't go on her own strength and determination forever. On her own, she couldn't make the marriage work. On her own, she couldn't make her anger go away. On her own, her power only went so far.

What's more, suffering in silence only made everything worse. When she planted herself in the church body, she took on part of its power too. She received support, encouragement, and unconditional love. And when she took part of the bread of communion, she took part of Christ's body, Christ's power. She laid her own dead sin and anger on the altar and held on to her own kind of resurrected life.

Her gratitude to God gave wings to that new life.

Writing down her specific blessings built an arsenal of thankfulness. It composed a gratitude symphony, and Sherri discovered how grace notes crescendo so that no matter how dark the night, she could always hear the music.

No matter how dark the night, she could always find a window and see hope.

And looking out that window, Sherri, you, and I see and feel the light and know deep inside: *finally, a change I've longed for.*

Prayer

Dear Father God, thank you for giving us Jesus, your beloved Son who knows what it is to feel the squeeze of tight spaces—yet also shows us that the only way to see and feel the light is to give thanks. Thank you that like the Israelites in the desert, though we may be uncomfortable, we are still comforted because your presence goes before us. And thank you that like you did for Moses, your hand protects us from that which we can't handle. Please open the eyes of my heart not only to say all the right thankful things but to feel thankful too—even when it hurts. Especially when it hurts. In the wondrous name of Jesus, amen.

7

Handing Over the Hand-Wringing

The best evidence of our having the truth is our
walking in the truth.

Matthew Henry

When I am in the practice of giving thanks and believing God means what he says, my soul quiets and my spirit thrives. My hands go about their work and don't tremble. But then the winds of change blow just a little harder and meaner, and I forget all I've learned, seen, and held dear in faith. At those times the enemy sees a keyhole-sized opening in the door of my heart and takes the opportunity to bust it down altogether. Before long, I'm buying into what he says more than what God says.

Sometimes I flat-out get tired of helping the enemy bring me down. He wants to make a mess of my business, and instead of purposely fighting him back, I unknowingly play along.

I play along by believing the lies he whispers in my ear about my identity. *You're hopeless! You're stupid! You're such a loser!*

I play along by following him away from Christlike behavior. *Go ahead and tell her off! She deserves it!*

I play along when change comes and I believe him when he says this time, it'll get the best of me. *You don't have what it takes to survive this. Just give up already!*

Whether I crack under repeated pressure or crack because I'm in a mood and it doesn't take much, my human weakness will leak through the fractures eventually. I may be able to get by on my own strength for a bit, but I have my breaking point just like everyone else. My breathing gets shallow, I start wringing my hands, and I want to throw things, cry, or cuss.

The point of our breaking points? They are the perfect place for Christ to come and be what we cannot. They are the perfect place for us to remember we have a Savior who identifies with our weaknesses. He is not unfamiliar with what makes us wring our hands with worry. "For we do not have a high priest who is unable to sympathize with our weaknesses, but one who in every respect has been tempted as we are, yet without sin" (Heb. 4:15 ESV).

Jesus knows weakness, he's felt weakness, and he isn't turned off by our weakness. He looked every weakness in the eye when he hung on the cross. And three days later when his eyes opened wide and his lungs inhaled oxygen, he conquered each and every one. In his own new life, he offers us new life by way of unlimited access to his throne of grace. When change comes, why wring our hands when we can cling to grace? He is there for us in each and every time of need (see Heb. 4:16).

I want to open the windows in my room *today* and lean out for a look while taking a deep breath of Jesus's grace. I don't want to let the enemy slam the frame right down on my fingers.

I don't want to let the enemy slam the hope right out of my heart.

Joseph's life was chock-full of change's deepest turmoil, and one would think his hands would have been red and raw from intense hand-wringing. When we last visited him, he had just changed from being a man in prison to being a man of position: prince, chief advisor to Pharaoh, point

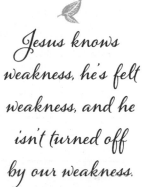

Jesus knows weakness, he's felt weakness, and he isn't turned off by our weakness.

of contact for all matters related to the country of Egypt. He went from the underground dungeon to the castle turret, another change of massive proportions.

But Joseph had been a man of position before and saw all that taken away from him. Sure, this change was favorable, but did he worry it could just as easily turn unfavorable again? Did he fret that somehow he'd find himself back in the basement? Or worse? I don't know, but I do know Joseph held on to God's promises amidst the highs and lows alike. Regardless of his job, position, and living circumstances, his actions were a fragrant offering. When he was sitting in a dungeon, he was looking to God. When he was hanging with Pharaoh, he was looking to God. Prisoner or prince, he kept his heart centered on God's will and let his life be a testimony to giving God glory. This was proven when his story continued a bit later in Genesis, specifically when his brothers, suffering from famine, came calling for food.

Because God told Joseph through Pharaoh's dreams to expect seven years of plenty before famine, Joseph wisely planned and saved food during the good years to feed the country during the hard years. During those seven years of bounty, Joseph stored up so much grain, it was "like the sand of the sea" (Gen. 41:49). The amount was so great, he couldn't keep records because it was beyond measure. It was a good thing too, because the famine affected not only Egypt but other countries too.

When the seven years of famine hit Canaan and families were starving, Jacob asked his sons to make the pilgrimage to Pharaoh's court in Egypt to get some grain. His sons obeyed, and who was the first person Judah, Simeon, Reuben, Levi, and the other brothers met? Joseph, the governor of the land who was also in charge of selling grain to its people. As Joseph undoubtedly looked very different in his Egyptian cultural setting, the brothers didn't recognize him. But Joseph recognized his brothers, and he was going to make them work for their grain—as is evident in how he treats them.

Upon meeting his brothers, he accuses them of being spies. He tells them they must go back and bring their brother Benjamin, who stayed behind with their dad, Jacob. While he provided his brothers grain for their families, he had one of them, Simeon, thrown in prison to ensure the brothers would return.

When the brothers made trip number two to Egypt with Benjamin, Joseph was visibly moved at the sight of his full brother (Joseph was half brother to all but Benjamin). Yet Joseph still kept his identity secret.

At Joseph's command, his steward played a trick on the brothers. He not only filled the brothers' bags with as much food as they could carry for their trip back home but also planted a "stolen" cup of Joseph's in Benjamin's sack.

After the planted cup was discovered in Benjamin's sack and the brothers returned to Egypt, Joseph gave his brothers a boatload of stress because he threatened to keep Benjamin as a slave as punishment for the "stolen" cup. The brothers knew if they failed to return home with Benjamin, their father would likely die of a broken heart.

Finally, Joseph couldn't keep up the game any longer. Years of emotional turmoil burst through as he cried out to them, "I am Joseph!" (Gen. 45:3). What he said after that blows me away:

> Then Joseph said to his brothers, "Come close to me." When they had done so, he said, "I am your brother Joseph, the one you sold into Egypt! And now, do not be distressed and do not be angry with yourselves for selling me here, because it was to save lives that God sent me ahead of you." (Gen. 45:4–5)

Yes, Joseph messed with his brothers and probably shaved a few years off their lives in the process. But when push came to shove, he showed grace and forgiveness in even greater proportions and ultimately did not let revenge have the last seat at the table.

Joseph let a God-given perspective have the seat instead. His ability to imperfectly but steadily make God-pleasing choices as well as dish out grace and forgiveness meant he had much practice at sharing an eternal outlook on anything and everything that came his way.

133

I wonder, if this had been me, would I have been so big picture–minded? So forgiving? I might have gone to greater lengths to take my frustrations out on the ones whose actions threw change at me in such drastic, negative ways. After all, I don't want their actions to get a pass. I don't want *them* to get a pass.

Head in the Clouds

Make no mistake: what happened to Joseph as a result of his brothers' actions was wrong. His family had several unhealthy habits—disrespect, favoritism, and pride, to name a few. But as entitled as Joseph grew up believing he was and considering all the poor choices he made out of that sense of entitlement, it was a terrible sin to throw him into the bottom of a pit.

To be sure, you can probably think about a pit you've been thrown into that changed your life. Divorce papers arrive to your reluctant palm? You're thrown into a pit. The one who was supposed to protect you uses you? Thrown into a pit. Your child rebels and turns his back on his mama's open arms? Thrown into a pit. Even though what happened to you was wrong as the day is long, perhaps you, like Joseph, can remember a distant poor choice (or several) that didn't do you any favors and contributed to your own disastrous results.

If that's you today—if you're wringing your own hands because you think you should have not said those words or not done that thing years ago—can I gently take one of your hands and walk you up the nearest hill for a little view?

Whatever the catalyst for the despair brought by change, look out in front of you and believe that the God who changed Joseph's pit of despair to a mountaintop of deliverance has in mind to do the exact same thing with your own. As the Lord convicts, go ahead and apologize to yourself, to God—and to others if necessary. We are all going to sin, but we don't need to sit in condemnation from that sin. God does not condemn, so you shouldn't either.

So what to do instead? Keep the same view as Joseph. He didn't waste time thinking about all the different choices he should have made. He didn't waste time blaming his brothers. *Instead, he spent his time giving credit to God.* Years after being thrown into the cistern, he could see that what God planned was to throw him into the chief role as the saving grace of Egypt—and as the saving grace of the same family who ignored his cries. Joseph's family may have been absent in his time of need, but Joseph could see that God was always present.

Such is the nature of God: what the enemy wanted to use for harm, God wanted to use to arm Joseph, his family, and a nation.

The younger Joseph might have lorded his position over them or punished them. After all, he had the power to do so, and his early dreams were prophetic as his brothers did indeed bow down to him. But Joseph didn't. Full of forgiveness and empty of I-told-you-sos, Joseph reassured his brothers as he generously offered them an abundance of food and land. Even though he still remembered his brothers' careless actions, he cared for them in return.

It's amazing what a little time and perspective do to one's own heart. Indeed, Joseph's drastic, tumultuous change brought about a great deliverance of more than one kind. God used it as a saving grace for nations of many people, and in the process, Joseph couldn't help but experience a changed heart as well. And out of that changed heart, Joseph uttered one of the most gracious statements recorded in all of Scripture: "You intended to harm me, but God intended it for good to accomplish what is now being done, the saving of many lives" (Gen. 50:20).

Would Joseph have picked slavery and prison time as stops on the way to redeeming his dysfunctional family? Probably not. But all along, he believed God had his best in mind and was able to see that empty cistern for what it was: a cocoon of rescue.

Your Sword in Hand

I can't wring my hands if I'm holding something in them.

When Ephesians gives us the rundown of the armor of God, the only non-defensive tool mentioned is "the sword of the Spirit, which is the word of God" (Eph. 6:17). Do we have any idea that the tool at our disposal has the power to fight off the enemy's tricks—to make him wish he'd never messed with us in the first place? God's Word is as effective at obliterating lies and darkness as a sword is at obliterating flesh and blood. It's a weapon that can cut our enemy off at the knees. It's a weapon that can loosen the clods of all the muddy, mucky feelings change brings.

But in order to have the advantages of the sword of the Spirit, I actually have to *use* the sword of the Spirit. What good is it just hanging out in its sheath at my side? What good is my Bible just hanging out on my bookshelf?

I am at a place in my life where I can 99 percent guarantee I will wake up before my kids to have a little Bible time. Since two of the three are teenagers, they usually don't get up until the last minute they have to. So, when the house is quiet, I get up and have a little quiet time. The goal is to read Scripture and my devotions, to give time to the Good Book before Facebook.

And here's where you mamas of littles slap your knee and laugh out loud. I know what you are saying: "Well, Kristen, goody goody gumdrops for you. That is one luxury I just don't have." Oh man, do I ever get that. I remember those days when my only quiet time was the first thirty seconds of a shower, if that. I remember pulling some major scheduling acrobatics just to get a little Jesus time in during *Blue's Clues*. Even then, distractions pestered me from all directions. Whether one of the kids wanted milk or the phone wanted answering, All the Important Things vied for my time.

But here's the thing: even this mama with big kids still faces distractions. Notice I said my goal in getting up early is to read Scripture. That doesn't mean it always happens. I sit down with good intentions to really focus on the Word, and sometimes that goes well. But other times, I oversleep. I try to do it while the kids are at school, and I forget about that PTO meeting and doctor's appointment. I am distracted because dinner needs making, blog posts need writing, and groceries need purchasing. All my responsibilities are written in capital letters and still vie for my time.

The moment my heinie hits our sofa, my mind is hit with distractions. It travels toward any number of things I must complete, such as folding laundry, finishing dishes, or running errands. Pretty soon ten, fifteen, twenty minutes have ticked by, and I can't remember focusing on even one Bible verse. It may not always be the kids distracting me (although sometimes it is), but it's always something. And from what I understand from my empty nester friends, the interruptions never leave even though your kids do. Distractions are always there, eager posers of emergencies and never on vacation.

I can't deny, however, that the days I am breathing in the Word, I am breathing out a better day. I can't deny that my internal compass resets and I see myself in relation to God's plan. I can't deny that I more accurately see myself positioned within my change, not overly important or underly valued, but as I am in reality.

Sure, it's easier to fall into Scripture in the middle of hand-wringing seasons. But if I am more intentional about reading Scripture during the seasons of plenty, I discover, like Joseph, that I am able to feast on it during the hard seasons. I don't need to wait till the famine to get to work.

The days I am breathing in the Word, I am breathing out a better day.

Of course, no day is a bad day to have my sword ready!

I find it comforting that no matter the season we find ourselves in, our time of soaking up Scripture doesn't have to resemble any particular model to be good for us. Soaking it up on any level is always best for us. A sit-down quiet time? Awesome. Reading Scripture on your Bible app while in line at Target? Fabulous. It will all seep inside and start to make a difference.

I see this reflected when I remember my sweet, chubby James as a baby. He gave me a beautiful picture of what it looked like to feast on Scripture every time he sat down to eat. Like many babies and toddlers, my James was a boy who liked to experience food rather than simply eat it. I would place him in his high chair, snap on the tray, and watch as his round arms and legs bounced up and down with anticipation and excitement. He knew what was to come. Spaghetti! Chicken and rice! Applesauce! Blueberries! It didn't matter—he was getting to ingest and explore some really yummy, amazing stuff!

Within minutes of placing his food in front of him, it looked like James's goal was to smear the food over every square inch of his tray and body. From time to time I saw him take a fistful of food into his mouth, but more often I saw him take a fistful of food and smear it over all points within reach. He had no awareness that the eating part took priority over the playing part. By the time he would be finished, I'd look at the noodle- or rice-painted scene and say to him, "Did you actually get any of this inside you?"

Well, obviously he did. As a baby and toddler, James did not hold the nickname "Hoss" for nothing. He was plump and healthy—the perfectly quintessential fat baby. Lots of food may have sloshed over the edges of his mouth and high chair tray, but enough of it made it inside him too.

I think Scripture reading for us is much the same.

Distractions elbow their way in on my time. Some of my Bible time gets sloshed over the edges and down the sides of my brain. But a lot of it sticks too, and I can't deny the evidence of God's truth working in my life. I feel Christ alive and active in ways I couldn't have imagined before. I still have miles and miles of room left for growth and improvements, but there are some things that consistent (even if distracted) time in the Word has turned from Very Big Things to a blip on my radar. I am better at giving credit to God for the highs as well as giving God credit for being able to handle the lows.

However, let's get real here: the Word isn't going to make you better equipped to handle change every single time you sit down to soak it up. That's okay. You don't need to come out with a brainchild or blog post every time you simmer in the Word. As Pastor Bryan from my church states, "God doesn't rebuke, he invites." And he invites us to soak in his Word with the understanding that it will *over time* contribute to your overall well-being.

There's one more reason the Lord invites you to hang out with him: because *he honestly, truly likes hanging out with you.* I love the words Robert Boyd Munger writes from the perspective of Jesus:

> The trouble is that you have been thinking of the quiet time, of Bible study and prayer, as a means for your own spiritual growth. This is true, but you have forgotten that this time means something to me also. Remember, I love you. At a great cost I have redeemed you. I value your fellowship. . . . Whether or not you want to be with me, remember I want to be with you. I really love you.[1]

Consistently dining on Scripture can't help but create a healthier soul. I want to do so regularly so that I regularly see the benefits, feel its wisdom coursing through my veins and its life racing through my blood. I want the voice of heaven to reach my heart. I want God's presence to carry me through every toilet-scrubbing, meal-sharing, carpool-driving part of my day. I want to feel him moving in my life during change's lush and lean seasons alike. Because then, as my son James proved, even distractions can't stop my scriptural frame from lookin' like a hoss.

Kicking Sass

If I absolutely, positively want to fully hand over the hand-wringing, what else can I do?

I can kick some sass into my prayer life by incorporating Scripture into my prayers too. I kick some prayers into action by praying the Lord's power against my fears.

A lot is said about the value of quiet prayers, words whispered in the corners of our souls in good times and bad. And to be sure, I am one to whisper prayers and be mindful of stillness with God. But even in the quietest of prayers, we can still get a little bold, brave, and sassy by wielding some God-given power before his mighty throne.

When we combine our prayers with Scripture, we hold a concoction that not only fights off the hand-wringing but blows the enemy right off the map. It's just one more way to keep our sword out of its sheath and use it like a pro, to decimate our fears by praying specific Scriptures out loud.

At the end of this book is a handy list of Scriptures that are rock solid truth for times of wishy-washy change. I take one such as the following and write it in my prayer journal, underline it in my Bible, or tap it into my iPhone:

> I pray that the eyes of your heart may be enlightened in order that you may know the hope to which he has called you, the riches of his glorious inheritance in his holy people, and his incomparably great power for us who believe. (Eph. 1:18–19)

And I pray this to God in heaven:

Dear Father,

You know how the fears loom regarding this difficult change. But your Word encourages us to open the eyes of our hearts to behold the hope that is you. This is my desire,

Lord. I desire for the eyes of my heart to be spotlights drawn to you so strongly that regardless of my circumstances, I see only you and your all-out goodness. You have prepared a glorious inheritance for me, Lord, and your power is for all those who believe in you. Help me believe that you are for me, not against me in this change. Search the corners of my heart for any unbelief and knock it out. I love you, Lord. In Jesus's name, amen.

When we incorporate God's Word into our words, we mix up a potion of superpowered proportions that is capable of killing any and all fears once and for all. It's exactly the kind of power Annie Dillard describes this way:

> Does anyone have the foggiest idea what sort of power we so blithely invoke? Or, as I suspect, does no one believe a word of it? The churches are children playing on the floor with their chemistry sets, mixing up a batch of TNT to kill a Sunday morning. It is madness to wear ladies' straw hats and velvet hats to church; we should all be wearing crash helmets. Ushers should issue life preservers and signal flares; they should lash us to our pews.[2]

We need to suit up, friends. We need to get a little serious and a lot intentional about making our posture match our power. So the next time change's fears try to invade your space, they will have no chance to become comfortable because you are going to put your Scripture time and prayers into action. You are going to infuse your prayer life with power from heaven itself so you are prepared to walk through your change with obedience.

Girls, let's be prepared to kick some sass.

Allison's Story: When Your Heart Wrings as Much as Your Hands

More than anything, Allison wanted to be a caring and compassionate mom. Having grown up in a home where family members treated her unfavorably, all she knew was her own desperate clinging to the adults in her home and the adults' utter dismissal of her in return. So when she and her husband, Scott, discovered they would soon be parents themselves, she didn't want to perpetuate the idea that their children were unwelcomed or outsiders in their own home. She desperately wanted to parent a different way so her children could live a different story.

As a young mother, Allison heard a pastor say that when it comes to parenting children, "you don't mold them but unfold them." This truth deeply resonated with Allison, and it served as a reliable guide for lovingly nurturing her children while still graciously allowing them to find their wings.

But then God threw her a curveball with her firstborn—a curveball that would challenge that premise and cause her to want to mold rather than unfold her child all the days of his life. Her son Nathan—her "gift," as the name means in the Hebrew language—was born with Asperger's syndrome, a form of autism. Slowly, Allison's pretty thoughts of the unfolded inner child turned into anxious dread under the weight of a hundred terrifying questions. *How do you unfold a child who is born "without the social gene"? How do you unfold something that's missing? Will he ever have a friend, a girlfriend, or a wife?*

When Nathan's diagnosis was determined at three years of age, Allison fell into a depression. She bought the enemy's false bill of goods that said this diagnosis meant her son would never amount to much. The enemy whispered lie after lie to Allison, and each one screamed at her mama heart: Nathan would remain friendless, never get married, and eventually become a nuisance to society. In her devastating depression, Allison had visions of the earth opening and swallowing her as she contemplated every dream envisioned for her son vanishing.

With her heart feeling every bit as squeezed as her wringing hands, Allison turned to Scripture and learned the only thing able to burn the false bill of goods was the fire of truth. Early on, the Lord called her to be faithful to him and to trust his Word, so she chose her Bible as her main parenting handbook. As new seasons came and she found herself in need of fresh inspiration in parenting a special needs child, the Bible became her go-to book for help. She dove in and discovered a feast of hope as well as rock solid truth that helped her keep her wavering emotions in check. Even though Nathan developed more slowly than his peers, God's faithful follow-through in his plans for her son was made available right on schedule.

Time moved ahead and Allison parented well, largely able to hand over the fears about her son to Jesus. However, when Nathan turned eighteen and left her daily presence for college, some of the worries pursued her with renewed vigor. While experiencing a child's transition to adulthood is a difficult period for the most seasoned of mamas, Allison had to fully, completely give up the familiar lies that said her son would have troubles without Allison there to care for and guide him. She had to embrace the scary unfamiliarity, healthy though it may be, by believing God's promises of provision, favor, and blessing for her son were just as present now as when he was younger.

During that emotional time, Allison felt she was tossing her son into the deep waters of the real world. While she and her husband had done their best to teach him to swim, she knew part of the unfolding was believing God would continue to show Nathan how to fully develop into all God desired for him. She knew repeating patterns of clinging to her son too tightly could risk losing him. So with her husband's patient help and wise counsel, she began to let go and let God finish his work in her boy.

By no means was this easy. Because of her difficult relationship with her extended family, Allison feared that purposely embracing this change—letting go and trusting God to fully unfold her son—would bring distance in her relationship with Nathan. But through Allison's consistent time spent in Scripture, God graciously reaffirmed his promises for Nathan in her heart. She discovered a deeper level of the Lord's faithfulness as she fully realized she could trust God to be an always attentive, always present Father to her son.

The evidence of God's presence in this change lingers in everyday, beautiful ways. Allison and Nathan have a close, thriving relationship. She gets to witness her son's interactions with good friends. He goes on dates and maintains a job while earning straight As in college. But most importantly, the evidence of God's presence in this change made room for Allison to see something emerge in Nathan's heart she had missed before: an utter and desperate need for God that is so tangible, she sees it changing the landscape of his life while capturing his soul.

Fully releasing her tight grip on this change released her son into the care of Christ. Even as she felt the bittersweet realities of sending her child off to college, she knew her ability to keep an eternal perspective—and keep the sword of the Spirit out of its sheath—helped her son to thrive and her mama heart to thrive too. As with any close loved ones, things aren't always easy or without challenges within Allison's family. But day by day, God continues to unfold his faithfulness to her son . . . and to her.

We make a daily decision to not let those fears determine our actions.

Letting go of the fears and lies that cause our hearts to hurt and hands to wring is not a once and for all activity. Rather, it's a daily choice to make, a daily remembering that *yes, God will be faithful here too.* We make a daily decision to not let those fears determine our actions. I love this portion of Romans that quotes from Isaiah:

> Careful! I've put a huge stone on the road to Mount
> Zion,
>   a stone you can't get around.
> But the stone is me! If you're looking for me,
>   you'll find me on the way, not in the way.
>
> 9:33 The Message

On one hand, Nathan's Asperger's is a stone in the road, a stone that complicates his life's journey. But on the other, Nathan's Asperger's is the means God uses to reveal his glory. And it's the means by which God provides unabashed love for a precious son and deep healing for a hurting mama.

The more we revel in Scripture, the more we are able to see *all* the stones change brings to our paths as looking glasses of God's love and favor. And the more we are able to see ourselves at peace in those looking glasses.

And maybe beginning to thrive too.

The Games are Won, Folks

As you now know well, my daughter and I are big gymnastics fans. In 2012 we watched with bated breath as the USA gymnastics team competed in the Olympic team finals. We did our best to ignore the spoilers all day, and so when the competition aired that night, we were chock-full of nervous energy, barely able to stay in our seats. After the vault, bars, and beam rotations, Russia had the lead in the overall standings. It all came down to the floor routine. Russia's team suffered several mishaps on floor while the girls on Team USA performed each routine flawlessly. The stellar performances were enough to put USA on top of the podium and into the history books. Upon hearing the standings, Faith and I jumped up and down alongside the rest of America.

Now, a few years later, when Faith and I find ourselves in a mood to watch something, we often choose to snuggle up with YouTube videos. Here and there, we rewatch the USA team members perform those floor routines. But every time we watch? It's a whole 'nother experience from 2012. Gone are our wringing hands and anxious hearts. In their place sit warm comfort and satisfaction that everything does indeed end well for America's team.

As a Jesus-believing sister, you have the exact same assurance. No matter the change that sits in your lap, you know things will ultimately end well. *The games have been won.* The outcome of your own kind of change games is as confidently won as the gold medal was for the gymnasts. No need to wring hands and sweat outcomes. Jesus won it all for us the moment he walked out of the tomb after dying on the cross. Jesus not only conquered death so you may have everlasting life in heaven, but he conquered death so you may live life to the full *right here, right now.*

Bravery is not the absence of fear but following God through the fear as you believe God's promises. It's holding on to the facts of our faith more tightly than to the fears for the future, like Allison did. It's believing change is not *in* the way of God's plans for us but *on* the way.

Let's hold tightly to the truth of Scripture and walk boldly through our fears as we give our wringing hands a break. Hold on to your sword, but also hold on to your confidence.

Because of Jesus, you have already won.

Prayer

Dear Father, you know my struggle with fears that make my hands wring and my nights long. Whether it's new ones falling in my lap or old ones revisiting the corners of my mind, give me a consuming passion and deep desire to fight the fears with the facts of your truth. May your unwavering peace chase them far, far away. When I feel fearful, may I rest hopeful. May I remember that anytime, in any place, I can approach your throne of grace. You listen attentively and care affectionately as you equip me to handle change appropriately. May I see my change not through the lens of fear but through the lens of your care. Thank you for sending Jesus as a guarantee that no matter the battles I face, I've already won. I love you! In his unchanging name, amen.

PART 3

Adapt

A Heart That Thrives

8

Because We All Need Friends in Low Places

My friends have made the story of my life. In a thousand ways they have turned my limitations into beautiful privileges, and enabled me to walk serene and happy in the shadow cast by my deprivation.

Helen Keller

In 1959, seven women were plucked from obscurity and ushered into the world's spotlight when their husbands were chosen to be America's first astronauts. Rene Carpenter, Trudy Cooper, Annie Glenn, Betty Grissom, Jo Schirra, Louise Shepard, and Marge Slayton met change in a way few people have. These wives and moms went from being regular military wives to being the faces behind the men of America's new space program. They went from being ordinary women to being cover girls featured in *Life* magazine. They went from blending in on ordinary air force, navy, and marine bases to standing out in neighborhoods that were a destination of reporters and tourists alike.

As wives to test pilots and fighter pilots who also flew dangerous missions in World War II and Korea, these brave women weren't strangers to fearing for their husbands' lives. But knowing your husband is going to be shot from the tip of a tin can rocket into outer space? Well, it's not difficult to understand why chain smoking became a common pastime for many of these wives.

Of course, not all the change was tough to embrace. The wives went from stretching a tissue-paper thin $7,000 a year military pay to earning a paycheck fattened up by several thousand dollars. They went from having tea with the ladies from the officers' wives' club to tea in the White House Rose Garden with Jackie Kennedy. As always, the good came with the difficult. But if there's one thing these women and the wives of later astronauts believed, it's that they wouldn't have made it through such drastic change without the support of one another.

As history played out for these original reality housewife stars, many of the women experienced overwhelming tension and heartache from pressures associated with the space program. These pressures wounded and widowed some of the wives. Some marriages survived the stress; some broke from it. All of the wives at times found themselves sitting in the lowest of low places.

And all of them found friendships that helped pull them out. It's not just words from a country song: we *all* need friends in low places.

In spite of all the nail-biting tensions and changes, some wives look back on that period with an especially strong fondness and nostalgia. Marilyn Lovell (whose husband, Jim, flew the famed Apollo 13 "Houston, we have a problem" mission) said this when reflecting on her friendships forged during that time: "Just talking about these friends—we all had such a good time in those days. . . . It was a time in my life that I would never give up. It was the best time in my life."[1]

All the changes Marilyn and the others endured were difficult, but they made it through because of one glaring positive in their lives: friendships. Friendships were a key ingredient that helped these women adapt to the changes this stressful lifestyle brought.

Let's face it: we don't need to be married to an astronaut to experience some level of stress in our lives, especially the stress brought on by change. Quite often, my ability to accept and thrive through change is directly proportional to the state of my near and dear friendships.

> Quite often, my ability to accept and thrive through change is directly proportional to the state of my near and dear friendships.

When I hopscotch across the Gospels and read how Jesus—the perfect Son of God—walked this planet's dusty, rutted roads with friends, I realize perhaps knotted-up, messed-up Kristen needs to do the same.

The Bible's words about friendships are some of my most favorite. For example, Ecclesiastes 4:12 offers a familiar image: "By yourself you're unprotected. With a friend you can face the worst. Can you round up a third? A three-stranded rope is not easily snapped" (The Message).

Safety in numbers—it's not just for the military. Seasons of hard change are not for pulling off alone, keeping company with only you. Like a lone animal in the forest, doing so leaves you vulnerable and unprotected.

What Friendship Provides

Change itself can come around and take something away, leaving a lonely space where there wasn't one before. If you're like Allison and just sent one of your children to college, the empty seat at the dinner table is a reminder of the loneliness change brings. If you're like Sherri and just went through a divorce, the empty place in your bed is a reminder of the loneliness change brings. So soldiering along through it alone is like fighting a shadow that looms twice as big in front of you. Without someone with whom you can share your feelings about this season of your life, that lonely space feels bigger than it really is. That lonely space feels lower than it needs to.

Friendship is more than an antidote to loneliness. Friendship is a strong cure that helps us walk up, down, and through the changes life brings. Friends are one way God heals the wounds and difficulties brought on by hard change. Friends make the hard days more manageable because they walk the winding roads with you. And friends who have gone through your kind of change before provide a model and valuable perspective for how to maneuver through it yourself.

No matter a woman's season of change, it matters that she has friends.

Visit the Islands, Don't Be One

As one who formerly lived on an island, I assure you it's a dreamy place to visit in the physical sense. But in terms of sisterhood, it's a dreadful place for your soul to permanently inhabit.

The other day, my dear friend Mary sent a Facebook message to some mutual friends and me asking us to pray for her. She was writing to share the news of her pregnancy as well as to ask us to pray for some upcoming tests she would undergo that would determine the health of her baby. In the past, Mary has had a difficult time carrying all of her pregnancies to term—she has learned the hard way that each pregnancy is an act of faith and dying unto oneself. But she could already feel the icy fingers of worry creeping toward her, and she wanted her sisters to pray against the fears and worries that threatened to overwhelm. In the message, she wrote, "Hopefully I will have good news to share, but if the news is bad, *I don't want to walk that path alone.*"

Mary didn't want to carry the burden of unfavorable test results by herself. Of course, as her friend, I didn't want her to carry it alone either. And in God's design, she's not supposed to.

We are infinitely more comfortable doing something new or difficult with others, so when others travel our road of change with us it bolsters us in body and spirit. No matter how deep the trials brought by change, friendship lifts the spirit as it refreshes the soul (see Prov. 27:9 The Message). It makes the weary one able to take one more step forward, handle one more setback, have one more test completed, write one more word down. It provides confidence in human form, grace from God's hands.

Most of the time I can stammer and stutter out words to heaven, and prayers from friends fortify my own words and actions. Sometimes, though, I wanted to pray for my own situation, but I was too worn out, too tuckered out to even utter a word. During those times God used faithful community members to take my place in the batting lineup when I didn't have the strength to stand at the plate. When I was too weary to pull the words from my heart, God used friends to pull them out for me.

God wants us to have friends and fellow sojourners who see us as he does. So when we think we might not make it through, these encourager-warriors know the potential we have inside and urge us to carry on in God's will for our lives. They not only urge us to thrive, they also take our hand and lead us toward a better way to do so.

Been There, Done That Kind of Help

We need community with others who can assure us we aren't the first ones to endure this kind of change as well as those who will assure us that *yes, you will make it through.*

I live in the same town as the United States Air Force Academy, one of a small handful of rigorous federal service academies spread across the country. While my air force husband is not a graduate of the school, he taught cadets there and was constantly amazed at the workload carried by them. We have had cadets at our house for dinner, and they filled in the blanks with crazy insider stories of the daily determination it takes to succeed there.

Before a cadet steps foot on campus, he or she must go through a rigorous application process that requires high academic standards, demonstrated leadership skills, and a nomination or two from a member of Congress. In spite of all the work that goes into getting accepted, many students who are accepted still drop out during their first summer of intense training known as "beast."

When I asked one of the cadets, Josh, to tell me what was the biggest factor in his making it through beast, he said without hesitation, "My fellow cadets, the friends I made there."

I find it fascinating that he didn't say, "I made it through because I was in shape" or "because I had mental discipline." While those two factors likely played a part in his success, Josh heartily believes it was his friends who most helped him through.

Community grown from shared adversity forms a bridge that allows one person after another to cross from one challenge to the next. It is the way we grasp a realistic perspective on our change and see that we aren't the only ones who have faced it. Scripture calls us to bear one another's burdens so we may fulfill Christ's law (see Gal. 6:2). That's because where relationships and Jesus are involved, a burden shared with someone else's similar burden divides the load for each person. Jesus will use friends to halve our troubles and burdens.

Naomi's Story: Opening Your Heart to Be Served

A trio of widows huddled together in the country of Moab, three women left without the mainstay of support: men (see Ruth 1). The death of Naomi's husband and two sons all but sealed the deal on a hopeless situation, especially since her two daughters-in-law were childless. No signs for a promising future were anywhere on the distant horizon.

What did lay in Naomi's hands and vision was evidence of being left outside the Lord's covenantal redemption. After all, her sons had gone against God's law and married foreign women. Even if God wanted to turn her situation around, why would he? Naomi tasted the bitter reality of a bleak outlook and had her name changed to Mara, meaning "bitter."

Sometimes change leaves us bitter and we wear it like a name, shaping and defining us.

Naomi didn't want her young daughters-in-law to share in the bitter situation, so she desperately tried to talk both into returning home to their own families so they could remarry.

One daughter-in-law, Orpah, finally relented and left to rejoin her family. The other, Ruth, clung to her mother-in-law.

Having suffered through her husband's death, Ruth knew the loss that comes with change. But she also knew this wasn't the time to endure it alone. By clinging to Naomi, Ruth took part in sharing the burden and therefore lifting it for each grieving woman. What's more, in clinging to Naomi, she clasped on to Naomi's faith. And in clasping on to Naomi's faith, she clasped on to hope that this loss was not the end of their story.

With care that spoke of her love for Naomi, she pleaded, "Don't urge me to leave you or to turn back from you. Where you go I will go, and where you stay I will stay" (Ruth 1:16).

Vowing that not even death would separate them, Ruth showed a devotion that went well beyond the care of a daughter-in-law to a mother-in-law. Her devotion sprang from a God-placed desire to show deep love and to give wings to that love through actions that provided both women with a future of hope.

With Ruth's arms wrapped around her, Naomi had a choice: open her heart to accept Ruth's offer of devoted friendship or reject it altogether. Witnessing Ruth's determination, she chose to accept it, and from then on they handled their change together.

That is the blessing of a good friend: they outlast the protests. They stick close and refuse to let their friend go through their change alone. They see through all the "I'm fine" and "I'm good" statements to the heart of the matter and help where they can.

But we can't ignore the fact that ultimately, Naomi made the choice to allow Ruth into her life for the long haul. She chose to say yes to vulnerability, yes to letting her daughter-in-law do the gritty parts of life with her while she was at her lowest.

After traveling back to Naomi's hometown of Bethlehem, Ruth found a field in which she could pick up leftover grain left behind by the harvesters. As God divinely arranged, the field belonged to Boaz, a close relative of Naomi's. And as that close relative, Boaz was also a kinsman-redeemer. A kinsman-redeemer held the responsibility of preserving the family name and property. Preserving that could play out in various scenarios, one of which was to marry the widow of a deceased relative and therefore preserve that relative's bloodline. With favorable encouragement from Ruth, Boaz took the necessary steps to do just that. After he married Ruth, they had a son named Obed, who became the father of Jesse, who in turn was the father of King David. And from King David came the King of Kings: Jesus. Once again, the difficulties from change birthed unimaginable blessings, this time due in part to an extraordinarily devoted friendship that sprang first from the grace of God and second from the actions of Ruth and Naomi. When Naomi's faith waffled, Ruth's was emboldened. Ruth was able to grab on to God's strength when Naomi's was weak. And when Ruth wasn't sure what to do, Naomi gave sound counsel. The actions of both women kept them alive physically and spiritually. And in return, the once-foreigner turned family member and the bitter-turned-hopeful mother-in-law were blessed to take part in the lineage of Christ.

God uses our friends to show us how to thrive through change. And when we keep our own hearts open to receiving those friendships, we pave the way for God to use that community as our own "kinsman-redeemer." Just as a kinsman-redeemer of biblical times took actions to preserve the family name, your community kinsman-redeemer takes action to preserve an accurate picture of yourself. As Bonhoeffer says about friendship, "Visitor and visited . . . recognize in each other the Christ who is present in the body; they receive and meet each other as one meets the Lord. . . . They receive each other's benedictions as the benediction of the Lord Jesus Christ."[2] In other words, community is a powerful way God's heart is made known to our own.

When you sit in the middle of change, a friend is one who assures you, comforts you, and holds you. When you don't know how to pray, friends become the words and actions of Jesus and prayers of the Holy Spirit. When you don't know what to think, they become an accurate perspective on your situation. They hold hands and hearts and are a light when you don't know which way to go. They are worth opening your heart up for.

The other beautiful part about opening yourself up to let others serve you? From the overflow of that blessing, you will want to serve others too.

Cheryl's Story: Opening Your Heart to Serve Others

Once upon a time, Cheryl married an all-around great guy named Keric who was also a very successful sales manager. Together they appreciated perk after perk of an income with wide borders, including owning a large home in the same neighborhood as a former president of the United States. Cheryl reaped the benefits of a live-in housekeeper and nanny who helped manage her home and care for her and her husband's two young children.

While Cheryl and Keric enjoyed the company of a wide circle of friends whose lifestyles mirrored their own, they couldn't ignore the growing inner turbulence calling them to do something radical in comparison to their current way of life. More and more often, they felt "alone in a crowd" and an ever-increasing difficulty meshing their inward values with their outward lifestyle. Their desire to "pull up stakes" and drastically change their situation was confirmed Sunday after Sunday at church when their pastor's sermon echoed Jesus's call to follow him. They *knew* Jesus was calling them to something bold and different.

After much prayerful consideration, Cheryl and Keric decided the right thing to do was for Keric to leave his lucrative job to join the US Air Force. They knew this decision brought a real possibility they would lose connections with friends who didn't understand their choice to change lifestyles. They knew Keric's job change might upset their family as well, especially since at the time the United States was building up to go to war with Afghanistan and Iraq. They knew Keric's income in the air force would be one-fifth of his current salary. And Cheryl knew she would have to say bye-bye to the comforts of a live-in housekeeper and nanny.

Sometimes you must leave the comforts of *what is* to embrace the potential of what *will be*.

But once they made the change, they also knew a great inner satisfaction and felt a keen awareness of God's protection over their family. While the many changes associated with Keric's new career brought much uncertainty to their lives, under it all lay a profound sense of peace that their family was in the middle of God's will.

Sometimes you must leave the comforts of what is to embrace the potential of what will be.

Once they became a military family, everything fell into place, and Cheryl felt truly at home in their new lifestyle. Cheryl attributes much of this peace to several factors, but at the top of the list was God's abundant grace in the form of meaningful friendships. For one thing, what both Cheryl and Keric felt was missing from their lives before Keric's career change was the presence of deep, genuine relationships with other couples and families. What followed from their obedience through the change was a level of friendship unknown to them before.

As Cheryl learned her way around the various difficulties of military life—namely, the absence of her spouse for long periods of time and of close proximity to her extended family—the friendships she formed were key to her thriving through this lifestyle change, she believes. While Cheryl and her husband navigated a new military life, they also navigated family life with two toddlers. Their friendships with families of similar ages gave them support in knowing how to maneuver the ever-changing waters of parenting. And when the difficult hours between naptime and dinnertime lingered, Cheryl's friends and neighbors gave her something to look forward to by way of a giant playdate in the cul-de-sac. When Cheryl became frustrated with the exhausting realities of balancing housekeeping, grocery shopping, and personal hygiene with two young children and a dog underfoot, her friends gave her support by way of listening ears and camaraderie.

Cheryl believes her friendships not only helped her thrive during her family's lifestyle change, but they helped give her a big picture view of her family's role in God's greater plan of helping others. To illustrate this, Cheryl recalls a story that took place in her early days as a military wife. On one evening in late spring, she found that every one of her new friends' husbands was traveling as well as her own. So as they gathered in the cul-de-sac for their afternoon ritual playdate, they decided to converge at Cheryl's house for dinner with whatever leftover tidbits were in everyone's fridge. Each wife had a sparse offering on her own, but when combined, the meal was a feast. The kids were all happy to eat and play together, and the moms were relaxed and able to enjoy an easier evening away from the stove.

Cheryl remembers how that one simple time together laid a cornerstone to a foundational belief that not only was community a powerful antidote to her major life change, it was a tremendous fringe benefit that helped her see life completely differently. She says, "Individually, God gives us each talents, but pieced together with gifts he's given others, we become something bigger, better, and more fulfilling than what we could be by ourselves." And together, those friends serve to double the joys and halve the sorrows in a math equation only

God could orchestrate. Cheryl's friends became her Aaron and Hur and held up her arms as she grew weary (see Exod. 17:12), but they were also her Ruth-sisters who shared in her joy by celebrating her victories (see Ruth 4:13–15).

Because of the sense of peace she found following her obedience through the change, Cheryl had the ability to focus on the people around her family and more intentionally interact with them. Cheryl served love on a plate when she invited people over for one of her fabulous meals that could put a Food Network chef to shame. When a neighborhood mom needed help with child care, she watched her children for her. When the temperatures soared in the hot summer months, Cheryl dropped off a perfect tall glass of sun-brewed sweet tea topped with fresh mint to friends and neighbors.

Cheryl and her husband kept their hearts open to their neighbors and found that loving and serving them brought a fresh-air quality that didn't take away the difficulties brought by change but did allow their lives to flourish during it. It buoyed them on to serve their greater community at large too by volunteering at the local homeless shelter and becoming more active in their church.

In Lysa TerKeurst's book *The Best Yes*, she writes, "The one who obeys God's instruction for today will develop a keen awareness of his direction for tomorrow."[3] Cheryl and Keric proved this truth when they first obeyed and then followed God's leading toward a new lifestyle direction. I would also add that the one who obeys God's instructions for today also develops a keen awareness of God's fulfilled promises for tomorrow. And those fulfilled promises may look like a wealth of soul-fulfilling friendships that feed you in ways you never imagined.

How to Be a Friend to the One Going through Change

When Jesus sat in the Garden of Gethsemane the night before he was crucified, he asked one thing of his disciples: "Sit here while I pray" (Mark 14:32).

He simply wanted their presence, nothing more. No small words, no grand displays of emotion. Because as Jesus waited to endure the most harrowing trial any person has ever endured, he wanted only the comfort of presence in his affliction. Perhaps in that is the key to being a good friend to those going through change.

Just sit with them.

My dear friend Rebecca models this so incredibly well. If you are blessed to have her in your circle of friends, you are blessed to know the way she sits quietly with you. It's a beautiful thing to behold because as she sits with you, she holds no ulterior motive other than to simply *listen*. With her hands folded and lips closed, she opens her heart to receive what her friend has to give in the moment. Of course, a hallmark of good friendships is when both people get to do this from time to time. But if one person is going through a difficult season of change, the other must be willing to place her own words on an altar in one conversation or several and listen with abandon and intention. Like Rebecca, she must reconcile the fact that her and her big opinions don't need center stage for every conversation, particularly when her friend is going through a monumental change.

This isn't always easy to do. Being a good listener takes a real lack of insecurity and the knowledge that one friend's circumstances and victories in them don't diminish your own gifts, choices, and circumstances. It takes compassion to listen and know her struggles do not elevate your position in the imaginary Woman Who Has It Most Together competition. But more than that, it takes humility to put all parts of yourself on hold as you quietly but decisively put a spotlight on your friend. To the friend going through change, humility says, "I see you and what you're going through. Because you have such incredible worth to me, this part of your story is worth hearing too."

Humility is the heartbeat of all encouragement, and a good friend's heart pulses with it.

Humility is the heartbeat of all encouragement.

No one lived this more than Jesus. But it should be said that while a good friend sits and listens to her loved one going through change, this doesn't mean there is never, ever a time to speak up. When Jesus met the woman at the well in Samaria, he didn't completely ignore her living situation, which included a live-in boyfriend. But he didn't cover their conversation with condemning words either. (Of course, Jesus never condemns. He convicts, but he doesn't condemn—see Romans 8:1.) He waited for her to ask for truth, and after she did, he shared with her his wisdom, which included an accurate assessment of her situation.

The woman at the well had a heart willing to receive, and your friend may or may not share the same willing heart. Either way, that's okay. But if you sense her wanting your honest reflections on her season of change, then your only job is to obediently follow through. Because part of being the kind of Proverbs friend that loves at all times (see Prov. 17:17) is being the friend who loves through words that may sting but nonetheless are for her and not against her.

When human love guides our actions, we are more inclined to be the kind of friend who keeps her own selfish desires first. But when we love with spiritual love, we see the other person as Jesus does—someone crafted in the Father's likeness and stamped with his approval. So whether we agree or disagree with how they handle something, we remember to treat her like Jesus would. When both friends keep this in mind, both friends can enjoy an orchard full of fruit.

By the same token, we girls must keep our expectations out of friendships. If we feel led to listen and minister to a friend going through change, the best thing we can do is not expect anything in return. We don't treat our time with them as an investment we assume a future profit on as much as a gift we give with no strings attached. We must strive to keep the heart of Jesus at the heart of our interactions and remember that the purest love serves and sacrifices rather than expects and demands.

What If I Know I Need Friends and Can't Find Them?

Bonhoeffer called the grace of community "the roses and lilies" of life.[4] But some experiencing change have discovered community can be the thorns and weeds of life too. Perhaps that's you. Women have hurt you, and as far as you're concerned, the only way to make living well through change possible is to keep your "friends" far, far away.

Undoubtedly, it is a tempting idea, and one that I've entertained too.

But alone is never the way Jesus asks us to go. So what are some ways you and I can get brave and invite others into our hearts and homes? How can we open our hearts to spend time forming friendships so that in the process we are better equipped to handle change as we serve others?

We do three brave things: *open up*, *show up*, and *lift up*.

First, we get brave when we *open up* our home to other people. Now, I'll be the first person to tell you this feels twice as brave because opening your home makes you feel twice as vulnerable. First, there's the idea that people coming over will see your dirt and judge you for it. It may feel that way, but women don't do that nearly as much as we assume they do. Besides, which kind of house makes you exhale a bit and relax—the kind dotted with messes or the kind buttoned up to perfection like a museum? I'll take the messy one, thank you very much.

Also, this feels especially brave because you could invite people over and they don't come. Let me assure you, if that happens, you will survive. How do I know? Because I've hosted a playdate and thrown a party at my house and had not one single person show up. *For real*. But more often than not, people did show up. We ate dinner together, talked together, watched our kids play Thomas the Tank Engine together, drank afternoon tea and coffee together, discussed interesting books and movies together, and got to know each other together. Have I become lifelong friends with everyone I've ever invited over for dinner? No. But have I developed a few near and dear friendships with some? Absolutely. And those friendships were worth every rejection or it-didn't-work-out I've ever received.

Second, we *show up* at places where other people are guaranteed to show up. For me, this looks like places that are crawling with women, like church and my kids' school. It means getting involved in just one small area at either place (or both) so I can get to know others. When my kids were small, this also looked like story time at either the library or Barnes & Noble. I met one treasured friend because we both kept showing up at our neighborhood park after our kids awoke from their afternoon naps. When I look back over the years, it's amazing to see how many women God placed in my path simply because I was standing on it.

Last, we *lift up* every single friendship concern to our Father in heaven. When I do it, I don't always use my sweet Sunday school voice. If I am going through a stressful friendship season, I have no problem being honest with God in my assessment of the situation. God is intimately acquainted with every inch of me, so he isn't shocked or put off by my real feelings. What's more, God truly desires for me to have community. So when I tell him my desire and it aligns with his, I know he'll answer my prayer in the way that's best for me.

It's Not You

If you look out your front window today and find your friendship landscape sparse, don't assume that means you're doing something wrong. And please, *please* don't assume it means there's something intrinsically wrong with you. Instead, assume it means that during this season, God wants you to focus your attention somewhere else. Perhaps this season opens up room for you to hang out closer to him or your family. Just keep taking your desires to his throne room. Keep talking to him *as your friend*. You never know what tomorrow may bring and who he may bring to your path.

The only way to guarantee never making friends again is to never try again. If I want near and dear friendships to help me thrive through change, I'm going to need to put in a little effort here and now. The fruit of that effort? Friendships of the highest good, given to help me when I'm at my lowest.

 *Prayer*

Dear Father in heaven, thank you for being an always present, always faithful friend in my life. You are the only One who provides never-disappointing friendship, and I thank you for it. Help me see myself as someone worthy of good, enduring friendships, and show me how I can bravely and wisely put myself in places to find genuine friends who love me well during all seasons of my life. Make me the kind of friend who not only opens up her own heart to be served but generously serves others as well. In the name of Jesus, who is a friend to all, amen.

9

Asking the Right Questions to Become Fit for the Right Purpose

If you keep in step with the Spirit, God is going
to make sure you get where he wants you to go.
He is always behind the scenes, engineering our
circumstances and setting us up for success.

Mark Batterson, *In a Pit with a Lion on a Snowy Day*

The thing about change is that it brings with it a truckload of expectations. And tacked on to any truckload of
expectations is a trailer full of questions.

"My family's in a good position to welcome another child.
Why can't I get pregnant?"

"I've been earnestly working hard and following through on all my work commitments for as long as I can remember. Why did I get laid off?"

"I've been a good wife to my husband. Why was I not enough for him?"

Change brings our expectations to light while simultaneously wiping them away.

Life comes and makes waves of demands, and you think you're holding on well. But out of the clear blue, a wave bigger than the rest places you in its shadow before collapsing over and knocking you down. It's not what you expected, so in order to make sense of it, you ask all the questions that rush over and through you along with the wave.

Change brings our expectations to light while simultaneously wiping them away.

Of course it's perfectly okay to ask the questions. But when we are asking questions from change, we sometimes need to change the questions we ask. It's not about "Why is this happening to me?" but "What is God trying to teach me?" and "What does God want me to accomplish during this change?" Asking the right questions provides learning opportunities that help us uncover what God is teaching us as well as what God is doing through us.

Esther's Story: When the Right Questions Bring Deliverance

In a manner akin to an Old Testament version of *The Bachelor*, Esther was handpicked to be the new wife of King Xerxes. But at her cousin Mordecai's instruction, Esther did not reveal anything about her (or Mordecai's) Jewish ancestry.

Haman, a high-ranking noble in King Xerxes's court, enjoyed all the privileges his position afforded—including watching others demonstrate respect and reverence to him by bowing down to him. So Haman was all smiles when the king commanded all those in his court to do just that.

However, Mordecai refused to obey this decree and bow down. It is unknown whether he refused to honor Haman in this way because of Haman's membership in a tribe that was an archenemy of Israel or for some other reason. Whatever the cause, he refused to bow down, and Haman refused to overlook it. When he learned of Mordecai's Jewish ancestry, Haman fumed. The book of Esther describes his following course of action as follows:

> Meanwhile, having learned that Mordecai was a Jew, Haman hated to waste his fury on just one Jew; he looked for a way to eliminate not just Mordecai but all Jews throughout the whole kingdom of Xerxes. (3:5–6 The Message)

So Haman convinced King Xerxes to destroy *all* the Jews.

When Mordecai and the other Jews in the area uncovered his plot, they wailed and wept so loudly that Queen Esther soon discovered her cousin's distress. She sent one of her royal representatives to find out the source of Mordecai's anguish, and he relayed Haman's plans for all the Jews in the king's provinces and urged her to beg the king for mercy for her people.

Queen Esther paused at this request; no one just showed up in the presence of the king. Since it was against the law for anyone—even his wife Esther—to enter the king's court without first being summoned, I can imagine all the questions she must have had:

You want me to do *what*?
Wait, are you sure you heard right?
Really, how can you ask me to do this?

If Esther was to approach the king without first being invited, she risked death. Initially, Esther didn't respond to Mordecai's pleas with assurances. She replied with facts and fears and reminders of what could happen to her if she approached the king's court uninvited.

Mordecai responded with a different perspective:

For if you remain completely silent at this time, relief and deliverance will arise for the Jews from another place, but you and your father's house will perish. *Yet who knows whether you have come to the kingdom for such a time as this?* (Esther 4:13–14 NKJV, emphasis added)

Esther questions the *outcome* of her actions.
Mordecai questions the *purpose* of her actions.
Nothing in our lives escapes God's attention. If he cares enough to know the number of hairs on our heads (see Luke 12:7), then he cares enough to reveal his vested interest in us through all circumstances. Just like Queen Esther's placement in the king's family was on purpose, where you are today with the people in your life is not random or by accident. God is a *purpose-full* God whose actions are always *full of purpose*. Therefore, when going through a change, the right questions to ask are those that question God's purpose for us in our season, in our place, and with our people.

Mordecai's question was all Esther needed to shift her perspective too. She asked her cousin and the other Jews in the region to fast and pray. Esther approached the king and in turn found mercy and favor. She ultimately became the avenue through which God's mercy and favor traveled to an entire nation of people living in that area. She bravely revealed her own heritage and Haman's conspiracy and saved the Jewish people from annihilation.

Esther's story shows how the right questions can lead to deliverance during change. They are arrows that point where to go instead of waves that keep us swirling in the spin cycle of uncertainty. The right questions reaffirm your trust in God because they remind you that no matter what, he is ultimately for you too.

Mordecai's question helped Esther see that while approaching the king is scary, it could quite possibly be the reason God chose her to be queen in the first place.

What about you? When you stand in front of the mirror and ponder your own change, could your own ability to thrive through it be enhanced by asking different questions too?

Instead of "Why can't I get pregnant?" maybe it's "What else does God want to give me?"

Instead of "Why did I get laid off?" maybe it's "What better job does God have for me down the road?"

Instead of "Why did he divorce me?" maybe it's "In what incredible ways will God bring healing and restoration to my life?"

The questions shift our perspective and show how we can adapt through change to become fit for a new purpose: thriving in our lives because we see ourselves as whole and complete through the lens of Christ. This might be easier to do if we all asked ourselves the question, "What exactly does it mean to thrive?"

Changing Our Definition of Thriving

I don't want to just survive change; I want to thrive through it. But if you're like me, you may have gone through life attaching all kinds of precious notions to thriving. If someone thrived, it meant that from where she stood on her quintessential front porch, everything looked spectacular. It might not have been perfect, but it flirted with perfection. She was happy. Content. Even thrilled with the way her life was going.

It wasn't until I stopped to actually read the definition of *thrive* that my notions for it did a loop-de-loop. According to my computer's dictionary, it means "to grow or develop well." How interesting that it doesn't say anything about being perfect, or even dang near perfect. It doesn't say anything about sitting atop *People* magazine's "Most Beautiful" list or having your kids make straight As in school or winning every award out there for your line of work. It certainly doesn't mean we are running sunny-faced, skippy-dippy through life with our head filled with Pollyanna clichés. *No, to thrive means to grow well*. And a big part of growing well is seeing change with the eyes of heaven and knowing that God will always, *always* use it for us. How does he do this? By using change to help us grow well too. Part of what that looks like includes becoming fit for a new purpose, one that is tailor-made just for you. One that fits you better and more beautifully than anything you could have picked up or bought on your own.

To thrive means to grow well

Becoming Fit for a New Purpose

Like most doctors' offices, this room is more sterile than cheerful. I've finally made an appointment to deal with a problem I'm having: a sudden urge to use the ladies' room *all the ever-lovin' time*. As I sit in the doctor's office, I cross my legs (of course) and lace my fingers as they rest on my knee. My twentysomething doctor asks me questions, then scribbles notes after I answer them. I swing my foot back and forth and scan the titles of pamphlets on medical ailments by my seat as I wait for his diagnosis.

He clears his throat. "Well, I believe you have what is called a spastic bladder. It's a common problem for women *in your age group*, especially women who've had children."

He says it kindly, but the words hang around me like a dark, scratchy scarf. I refrain from telling him that since I only recently turned forty, I've been in my age group for all of twenty minutes.

He prescribes me medication and makes other suggestions that will help calm my bladder down. I shake his hand and tell him I'm grateful for his time and help today. But as I leave his office, only one thought is on my mind: *I'm getting older.*

My body changes with each new birthday. So I ask myself, *Through this change, what is God trying to teach me?* And the answer comes before I finish formulating the question.

I am becoming fit for a new purpose.

How appropriate that is! When I look up Webster's definition of *adapt*, I read "make fit for, or change to suit a new purpose."[1] If God is calling me toward a change, it is so I can adapt. For it is only through adapting that I am able to move forward into God's provision and blessing of contentment in my circumstances, purpose in his plans, and a life that genuinely thrives—or grows well to live well. This is his entire purpose for allowing the change in my life in the first place.

As for the changes in my body, God uses them to point me to other ways I am changing for good. Is my body running as smoothly as it did twenty years ago? No. But through its changes I find new desires to intentionally eat healthy foods, to stop apologizing for needing rest, and to pay attention to my body's limitations and needs. Thriving is as possible today as it ever was.

Love First, Know Second

When I was an elementary school music teacher, my favorite age group of kids to teach were around second or third graders. They were old enough to be somewhat independent, yet they were still young enough to see the best in me and believe my motives in dealing with them came from a pure place. Teaching them was most enjoyable because the connections were right for us to truly delight in one another. They would ask me questions like, "Mrs. Strong, what fun stuff are we going to do today? Can we play the Orff instruments? Can we dance to Haydn's *Surprise Symphony* again?" Their bright eyes, round with excitement, would look up at me in anticipation. They were as generous with their good expectations as with their hugs.

It is not a stretch for me to see why God asks his grown-up kids to become like children (see Matt. 18:3). They are tenderhearted, easily delighted, and eager to listen. They easily forgive and with the right instruction easily ask for forgiveness too.

Robert Browning wrote, "Let us say—not 'Since we know, we love,' but rather 'Since we love, we know enough.'"[2] Children move through life with love first and "know enough" second. Children love first and then let their actions spill from that love. They love first and because of it adapt easily. Then they ask questions that model this trust built on love.

Jesus models this better than anyone, and his questions reflect it. When we read earlier about the woman at the well, we saw how Jesus loved her first and let his actions spill from that love. His first question to her was, "Will you give me a drink?" (John 4:7). A simple, practical question that led him to offer her living water not from the well, but from the well Source.

Because Jesus loved first and allowed his actions to be motivated by that love, he helped the woman at the well become fit for a new purpose too: sharing what Jesus had told her with all whom she encountered in her town. She had tasted living water and not only thirsted for more but was eager to have others in her circle of influence taste it too. She knew her personal life wasn't doing her any favors; nevertheless, sometimes we prefer to cling to unhealthy familiarity rather than change to a healthy unfamiliarity. But then Jesus comes in and makes a personal offer so attractive—his grace and mercy in abundance—the woman at the well immediately changes her perspective.

Jesus comes to you too, right where you are in the middle of your day, in the middle of your circumstances. No matter how change came to you—either by your own doing or by the doing of others—he asks you questions to change your perspective and woo you closer to the heart of him: "Would you accept that my love for you is so great that everything I do is for you? Would you place your faith in me by believing this change helps you adapt toward a new purpose?"

Perhaps we can thrive through change *because* of the change, not in spite of it.

Fullness in Christ because He Loves First

While waiting in the line at the cosmetics store with my makeup, I check email. I receive one and read it as the line crawls forward. A friend has written to say she's thinking of me and just wanted me to know. It had been a long, too-tiring week, and her words hit a tender part of my heart. I tear up right there in line and hug my eye shadow and mascara as I pretend to be overly interested in a display of sunglasses perched next to the snaking line.

There is something beautiful about being thought of, isn't there? When I think of all that hangs off everyone's plates—errands to complete, families to care for, responsibilities to follow through on—to know the Lord brought you to their mind is an amazing gift in and of itself.

At another time, I am traveling and away from my family. I talk with friends and colleagues, write words for my book and blog, and eat pie for my own happiness. Woven through every conversation, meal, and thought are my children's faces, their funny expressions and old-soul thoughts. Of course, some of their ornery qualities visit my mind too, but when I'm traveling I find it easier to dwell on their good points so much more. I especially recall my teenage son James's reply to me every time I tell him I love him. He tilts his handsome head, raises one eyebrow, and says, "Of course you love me, Mama. That's what *all* the ladies say." I know my children through and through, so they occupy my thoughts and plans through and through too.

A friend dwells on another and is compelled to send her a note. A mother dwells on her child and smiles at the memory. And then I think about how much the Lord must dwell on me. How much he dwells on you. If he knows you intimately— which he does—then he can't help but dwell on you. Every detail that you are composed of is always on his heart and in his mind.

He thinks of you and smiles.

I think we are incredibly shortsighted as to just how much the Father dwells on us. He loves you, and his Son and the Holy Spirit believe you are worth their prayers. Not only that, but the Father delights in giving his kids gifts that are good for them. Thriving through change is good for his children. His plans aren't for you to endure change white-knuckled and miserable. No, his plans are for you to use it for your benefit and for his glory. Knowing this in our bones helps us put our fresh perspective into action.

Let me emphasize an important point: the Father will give you what is good for you in that change. If you are thinking of creating a change that will feel good but is not in line with God's Word, then that is not a change he will honor. But if the change is good for you and in line with his will for you, he will happily move mountains to encourage you to thrive through it.

Since we've already learned how to ask better questions concerning change, we now have the ability to see our change with renewed perspective. And where we have new perspective, we have greater clarity about how God is using the change in our life to work for us.

He gives us fullness of good things and rules over that which tries to interfere with those good things. We see this in Colossians 2:10:

> In Christ you have been brought to fullness. He is head over every power and authority.

He is head over the authority that says there's no way you'll make it through the ups and downs of parenting changes.

He is head over the authority that says you will not survive your spouse leaving you.

We have everything we need to handle change because we have everything we need in Christ.

He is head over the authority that says this disease will get the best of you.

He is head over the authority that says there's no way to make it through your loved one's death.

He is head over every authority that is a fear stalker and hope stealer.

And he demolishes them all with a smooth swipe of his hand and fills the space with the flood of his love.

It's truth that needs to sink into our souls: *we have everything we need to handle change because we have everything we need in Christ.*

Generous God: For Your Benefit

When you're a girl from Oklahoma, country music swirls in your bones. At least it swirls in *my* bones. I grew up on a steady diet of Barbara Mandrell, the Judds, and Johnny Cash, and I am quite sure I'm all the better for it.

Naturally, our radio dial today finds itself on a country station now and then, and like my husband and me, our kids have their favorite artists too. Keith Urban, Brad Paisley, Lady Antebellum, and Rascal Flatts rank toward the top.

So when we learned Rascal Flatts would be making a tour stop in Denver, we thought purchasing concert tickets would be a particularly fun surprise for James, Ethan, and Faith. My husband made the purchase, and over a dinner of smoked pork, baked potatoes, and salad, we gave them the good news. To say they were elated would be an understatement. They hooted and hollered, and David and I patted ourselves on the backs for raisin' 'em right.

We began the countdown to the big night, and when it finally arrived, the rainy downpour couldn't dampen our spirits.

After we parked the car and showed our tickets to the venue representative, I followed my husband inside. Upon entering the outdoor arena, I became confused when I saw that he didn't immediately veer off to our usual lawn seats. Because if our family is going to fork out the money to see a concert, we always, *always* choose either the nosebleed or lawn seats. Why was David moving past the lawn?

Without a hint or a glance my way, my husband kept walking toward the front. And without a question voiced out loud, my kids and I kept following him. After showing our tickets to another venue representative, David finally ushered us to our seats *in the tenth row*. Speechless and slack-jawed, I just stared at him. When I could finally get my wits about me to speak, all I could do was shout, "Thank you!" over the loud crowd noise and blaring speaker music.

Not once in my life have I been so close to a live concert stage, unless you count the years I was actually on the stage in the orchestra. *We had a blast.* Yes, the rain fell on us in sheets, but our family was too busy dancing and singing to care. That night offered a downpour of memories this original Oklahoma girl won't soon forget.

As we sped down Interstate 25 late into the night toward home after the concert, I laid my head back on the seat and said to my husband, "Love, that was one of my favorite, most fun surprises ever. Thanks again for giving us this gift."

He replied, "You're welcome, baby. To be honest, I had as much fun giving it as you had receiving it."

In that moment, I realized that is how God views his generous hand toward us. He knows the talents we hold, the bents we move toward, the interests we are excited by, and the things we love. After all, he planted all those in keeping with our God-given character inside us. How much then does it absolutely thrill him to give us good things? How much then does his own generous heart overflow with so much desire for you and me that his hands move eagerly to release to us things that not only are for our benefit but may even be meant to surprise us in the most unbelievable, joy-filled ways?

I would have been perfectly happy to watch Rascal Flatts from lawn seating. But my husband changed our status quo to give us something more. What if I would have stopped him on the way to the front of the stage and insisted he had no idea what he was doing while pulling him toward lawn seating? Would I have still heard a good concert? Yes. Would it have been as good of an experience as it turned out to be? No. For once, this headstrong girl just followed her man without questions and saw what better things lay ahead.

I heard the music, saw the faces, and danced like a fool. Perhaps that is the reward of trusting the One leading us into new places. Perhaps that is the reward of hearing the earnest voice of God speaking these words through life's changes: *I love you madly and long to show you all the ways I love you.*

May you and I both quietly follow as we enjoy an up-close view of the show. And may our pleasure glorify God in the process.

Generous God: For His Glory

As a music major in college, I sometimes had to go through the torture of playing pieces from memory. Y'all, I can't begin to describe to you the nerves and fears this would ignite in me. Sometimes my fears would be so obvious that in order to get them to simmer down, more than one professor tried to talk me into taking medication. It wasn't so much because I was afraid of messing up my performance by playing it from memory, although I certainly tried to avoid that. My nerves were mostly because I was afraid one wrong note would change the good opinion others had of me as a musician. It was enough to worry about aspects of playing such as tone, phrasing, and pitch. But throw in playing notes from memory? *Ugh.* My hands get all sweaty just remembering it.

When I travel back to the college auditorium stage, I see myself standing in either a short or long black dress, hair pulled up out of my face. I see myself playing my instrument on stage left, the black grand piano accompanying me on the right. I hear myself fumbling sometimes, doing well at others. And those times when I didn't play so well, you know what? *I still made it through.* I learned my reputation as a musician couldn't change because of a poor performance or two. And I learned that practicing the process—standing on stage and just doing the thing—is one good way to practice bravery, a handy thing to have in your back pocket during any type of change.

But what did the most good for my anxious little heart was realizing my purpose on stage was not to give a five-star performance; it was following through with my talents to the best of my ability so Christ would get the credit and glory. This eased the burden as it made me relax and accept that I was not the end event but rather the instrument God used to bring about his purposes.

For my senior recital, I stood up and played Saint Saëns, Vivaldi, and Poulenc. I nailed parts, stumbled in others. But at the end of the concert, in that split moment of time after the last note rings out and the audience exhales before clapping, I heard my private studio teacher shout, *"Bravo!"* into the darkened auditorium. I let her *Bravo!* ring in my ears and settle in my heart. It made me smile for more than relief alone. It made me smile because even though my playing wasn't perfectly performed, it was perfectly brave. It made me tear up because she chose to honor me by celebrating the perfectly good moments that showed through that bravery.

The Italian word *bravo* originates (not surprisingly) from the word *brave*, although it also means bold. I love the word *bravo* because if brave and encouragement got together and had a baby, her name would be *bravo*!

When we realize our highest purpose through change is to glorify God, he gives us the brave encouragement we need to make it through.

None of us is going to do this life perfectly. But as we bravely move through our change with eyes on God rather than our performance, God is shouting *Bravo!* to us, especially when we use our own unique, custom-made-to-fit gifts for him.

Really, you and I have the same purpose through change that we have through seasons of calm familiarity: to praise the One who generously loves us first and does everything for us out of that place of love.

Do you hear that sound ringing in your ears? Let it settle in your heart.

Bravo, sister!

Prayer

Dear God in heaven, thank you that no matter how low the questions and concerns try to take me during change, your power in my life and authority over it go lower and wider. In my normal desire to answer the questions that come with my change, help me to do so in light of your planned purposes, not my own perceived outcomes. Lord, no matter how my circumstances appear, I know that you are for me always and this change is achieving a new purpose for me as well. Help me remember that you long to generously show me all the ways you love me. And may my first response to your incredible, all-consuming love be to glorify you in return. I love you, and I thank you for Jesus. In his glorious name, amen.

10

Settling in the Home Where Your Heart Thrives

But change doesn't feel scary anymore, not like it used to. It seems like I no longer view life as a slipping away but a slipping toward.

Jennifer Dukes Lee

I smile ear to ear while watching the video online of my friend Becky's son, Austin, throwing the first pitch at a Kansas City Royals game. But when the video footage shows the catcher clutching the ball and then taking off his mask, my eyes sting as tears push themselves up and over. For standing there in that Royals uniform is Austin's dad, Rob, home from a year-long deployment in the Middle East. Austin's jaw drops when he sees the face behind the mask, and he flies from the pitcher's mound to his dad's arms.

I've seen a hundred of those reunion videos and photos, and this one is my favorite (other than my own) because I know the family. More than that, it's my favorite because I can literally picture the entire family together again. *At home.* Rob's too-long season away is finally finished. Becky's too-long season as a solo parent is finally over.

Now, I know Becky well enough to know that she did a great job taking care of Austin and his sister, Madison, during that year when Rob was deployed. She consistently got them to school and baseball practice and dance lessons. She tenderly loved on them when they had raspy coughs and ran persistent fevers. She bought them new school shoes when they outgrew their old ones. She made the best of her situation by imperfectly but wholeheartedly providing a stable environment during uncertain times, one where her kids could thrive.

But if you asked Becky if she'd like to get along like that forever, she'd surely say *no thank you.* She wanted her husband home not just for his help with the dishes and the driving. She wanted him home to do what Rob does best: love his family up close and in person. Of course, whether he's inside their four walls or across oceans, Rob loves his people well. But there is a settling—a long exhale—when doting dad and loving husband is at home rather than away. Because Rob helps his loved ones grow well and thrive, his presence in their family is felt and needed. Regardless of their address on the mailbox, wherever the four of them are together is home, and at home they all hold each other.

There is a safe feeling in being at home where one is held.

Rob's presence *is home* to his family. My own favorite four people *are home* to me because home is never a where but a who. It's about my people, the ones I can settle in with and therefore thrive with. And just as I find safety and comfort in my family during times of change, I find safety and comfort in the heart of Christ during change too. As I hold on to those same feelings in Christ, I then know Christ's presence as really, truly home. It is he who holds all things together, so no matter the tilt and whirl of change in this world, I am held together because of Christ.

No matter the tilt and whirl of change in this world, I am held together because of Christ.

Whether I'm living in my favorite location or moving to a different one, he holds me together.

Whether my husband sleeps next to me or thousands of miles away, Christ holds me together.

If my extended family and I are experiencing tension, Christ holds me together.

If my child is showing signs of a mile-wide rebellious streak, Christ holds me together.

I am at home—safe and held because I'm alive in Christ.

Alive in Christ

The Message translation of John 15:4 begins with these three simple words:

Live in me.

It goes on to say, "Make your home in me just as I do in you." We can be at home in his heart because he welcomes us in. He has cleared the books and paper piles from the spot by the fire, poured your favorite hot beverage, and thrown open the door to welcome you. The invitation is there, and the kindness in his eyes assures you it is sincere. You don't even have to call or text first. The smile on his face and his arm around your shoulders say, "I want nothing more than to spend time with you right now."

If any doubt sits near you as you question his sincerity, remember this: for Jesus to endure all he endured on the cross means he will go to endless measures to spend time with you. *To hold you, listen to you, embrace you, cry with you, and love you to overflowing.*

There is nothing more costly in this world—or anything that shows more proof of true love— than giving one's own life for those one loves (see John 15:13). From Genesis through Revelation, the Bible points toward a love story starring everyday people like you and me and a Savior who loved us enough to die for us. We take our tired eyes and look up to the cross where we see all our sins nailed, including our sin of putting more faith in what we see in front of us than in the One who sees everything.

When Jesus died and rose, he put an end to death getting the last word. So my death thoughts—the dread, the fear, the I-can't-do-this feelings—don't get the last word either. I recommit and reconnect my life to Jesus. I re-plunge myself in the waters of baptism and come up holding on to new life, resurrected life.

Redemption is spelled out in grand ways and small ways alike from the beginning to the end of Scripture. Jesus is love in action, and everything he does springs from his love for us. Living in Christ means living in the freedom of that redemption every minute of every tired, change-filled day.

The more we live in Christ, the more we not only better thrive amidst unlovely people but better thrive amidst unlovely, changing circumstances too. Both Joseph and Esther lived this. We can imitate Joseph by trusting God and loving the people in our circle of influence where we can, when we can. We can imitate Esther by trusting God to hold us close even as we walk far outside our comfort zones.

Christ moves through your circumstances, sister, not in spite of them.

Living in Christ is available to us in *every* circumstance, not just here and there. But no matter how we forget or fail to live this out, Christ's embrace remains. Heaven knows that just like Joseph and Esther didn't perfectly abide in Christ, you and I won't either. Rest assured, we are wildly loved through our flaws, our tightly held concerns, our pauses and questions.

Jesus asks us to make ourselves at home in his love (see John 15:9). Think of your own best friend, adoring grandma, or loving sister whom when you visit, you can't help but exhale as you settle in on her comfiest, cushiest chair. You are at home there because you are at home in the love lavished on you by the homeowner. They don't see you as a guest so much as family, and their actions stem from this.

One of those people in my life is my friend Kim. She has lived in three different homes since I've known her, and it's been pure joy to hang out in each one. However, I have little memory of her decorating style and cleaning habits in any of them. As I curl up on her oversized sofa, I'm so busy soaking up her attentive conversation, I don't notice whether her floors are wood or laminate, whether her countertops are Formica or granite. I don't see chaos collecting in corners or laundry spilling from bedrooms. Kim is so busy pouring into the state of my heart, I don't think to invest my energy in judging the state of her home.

I am *at home* there because Kim listens, asks questions, and is attentive without secret agendas. I am *at home* there because she loves me well there. In her presence, my heart relaxes too, because it's safe and welcome, so I choose to *enter in*.

It's the same with Jesus. We are *at home* in him because he loves us well there. What's more, when we say yes to *enter into* his home, we also say yes to *enter into* the change he asks us to live. We are still loved, still at home. We're safe and cared for—we're okay.

Entering in is what Abraham did. God asked him to accept the change, and when he obediently went where the Lord asked, he *entered in. The Message* translates Romans 4:3 this way:

> But the story we're given is a God-story, not an Abraham-story. What we read in Scripture is, "Abraham entered into what God was doing for him, and *that* was the turning point. He trusted God to set him right instead of trying to be right on his own."

The last of the scales fall from my eyes and I think I might finally get in my bones how change is positive and always for me: because God is positively always, *always* for me. He wants to let me settle in and rest on the sofa as he takes the Kristen-story from my tight-fisted hands. He wants to rename it a God-for-Kristen story, and by entering in, I give him full permission to do just that. When change sets my world off-kilter,

I remember that God made the world literally off-kilter, tilted on its axis. So change that tilts is change that's natural. The world tilts at the angle he designed. If I want to feel steady in this tilting, changing world, I would be wise to simply lean into it.

If I want to feel steady in this tilting, changing world, I would be wise to simply lean into it.

I can lean into the God-for-Kristen story he wants to write.

I can grasp this, but if I am to really, fully thrive through change and transition, there is one more step I need to take. I must also accept his invitation to not just be a guest in the home of my heart, but actually be *the host himself*. I have to allow him to own it as he oversees all the ins and outs of caring for it.

Christ Alive in Me

I read this quote a long time ago, but I still think of it often: "If you're coming to see us, come without warning. If you're coming to see the house, call ahead."[1] *Yes and thank you and amen.* We all know how relaxing and straight up fantastic it is to have friends and family members who are too busy delighting in you to care about your dirt—they could care less about your sticky floors, cluttered hallways, and dusty bookshelves.

Those people are a breath of fresh air because they put people over places. They model Jesus because like Jesus, they want to be with you in spite of your mess. And sometimes maybe even because of it! I can even show that kind of person the upstairs "catchall" rooms with the closets piled high with clutter and know her opinion of me won't change once she gets an eyeful.

When I am settling in to the fact that Christ is alive in me, I realize I don't have to keep the piled sky-high, heaped-up messy parts of my heart hidden from him. He can have full access to do with it as he pleases.

I am then moved to ask myself, "Why not allow him full ownership of that cluttery closet right along with the whole shebang? Right along with all of me?"

In his booklet *My Heart—Christ's Home,* Robert Boyd Munger refers to Christ's ownership of my heart's home as transferring the title deed containing its assets and liabilities, condition, location, and situation from my possession to Jesus's.[2] It's signing it all over to him for eternity. It's fully leaning into him and the knowledge that no matter what, Jesus is dealing with it *for* me better than I ever could on my own. I relax knowing that I don't have to be the one managing everything. There is freedom and rest where control and worry once resided.

I love these words Jean Fleming writes of the benefits that come alongside this title transfer to Jesus:

> When he moves into a life, he comes with a truckload of blessings. I am blessed with every spiritual blessing in Christ. But I will not live a beautiful life in a fallen world unless I live in the FULLness Jesus won for me at the cross.[3]

During times of transition, I am still blessed with every spiritual blessing in Christ. With Christ's indwelling in my heart, I have every right to live in the freedom that was so abundantly won for me. I will remember Jesus on the cross and how he bled and died for me to have *fullness* of life in every single season, not just the ones that are smooth and uneventful.

I do this by opening the doors of my heart *and* by giving Jesus the key to keeping it all well maintained. I do this by keeping things simple and remembering that living by faith and not by sight is the way I walk the path in changing times. But I am still tempted here and there to swipe at the fringes of control, to see God as the guest I need to do things for. I need help in seeing God as the host in the home of my heart all the time rather than just here and there.

Simply Be

Y'all, I totally won the mother-in-law jackpot. She is golden, I tell you. When Bev visits my house, she washes and folds my laundry. She cooks in and cleans up my kitchen. She wipes the dust off end tables and the ebony painted piano. Bev loves on her people in nitty-gritty, practical ways, and she makes me doubly thankful I fell in love with her son.

While I can't deny that I spend time tidying up before she visits, I also can't deny I don't kill myself over having the dog hair swept off every cushion or dust bunnies cleared from every corner. I don't concern myself with going all crazy with cleaning because there isn't that expectation from Bev for things to be *just so*. Yes, she'll take out the broom or vacuum if she sees something needs tending to, but it's a secondary benefit of her presence, not a primary one. Her primary goal is to be a helper and an encourager. She is infinitely more interested in learning about what's going on with David's job, my writing, and her grandchildren's activities. During her visit, she takes over things in a way that isn't pushy or uncomfortable; it's relaxing and freeing, and it gives me a much needed, much appreciated break.

Because of this she allows us to simply be us—to *simply be.* It's a genuine treat to hang out with her.

I need to embrace the fact that this is Jesus's desire for me too. He wants to take over so I am allowed to *simply be.* Simply share my heart, my dreams, my fears, my dirt. But unlike Bev's too-short visits, he doesn't want to take over for a limited time. He wants to do it forever. There's no need, no desire for me to give side glances at my junk piled hither and yon. When I rest knowing he is the most attentive conversationalist around, I am allowed to do nothing more than soak up his presence. I am allowed to accept what he most wants to have: simple companionship with me. Because of this, it's a genuine treat to hang out with him.

I forget that Jesus only wants me *to be.* To be *with him.*

Jesus only wants me to be.

Simply being with God shows my heart's desire, something God sees and smiles over no matter how my fleshy mess makes me move imperfectly toward my goals. No matter how many times I get distracted and off topic. No matter how much I try to make it complicated. No matter how often I fall and land on my backside. He is glorified every time I acknowledge his presence.

The more I practice simply being with him, the more I am aware of his presence. So when change enters my life, simply being with Jesus helps me to spill open a bit more and then a bit more, allowing his comfort to enter the places change has entered. When life changes, I find myself still growing well.

I find myself thriving.

I used to believe that if change would stop finding me—and asking me to change with it—I'd be more content. Now I find contentment in knowing that God is using the change to change me for the better. To change my life for the better. The seasons glow and fade into the next, and the kids sprout and mature into new stages. I can embrace all of it, leaning into the natural order and goodness of it.

Leaning into that is leaning into hope that God's familiar promises come with change and transition. I don't just hold that promise of blessing in my heart.

I live it.

Home: Faith Is the Front Porch Light Left On

When I was pregnant with twins, my husband and I elected not to find out their gender before they were born. We loved the idea of embracing the surprise element right up until the end. While this refusal to take advantage of modern technology in obstetrics didn't complicate things greatly, it did mean we had to pick out two sets of names for each gender. This was an easy decision if we had one or two boys, as we knew we wanted to name them after our fathers and David's brother. But deciding on the girl names was trickier. First of all, my girl-heavy family offered a plethora of options. And being a lover of flowery names, I wanted the girls' names to reflect both flowery notions and family names. My husband and I finally agreed that the names Madeline and Makayla blended beauty and both those qualities well.

Delivery day came, and after giving birth to two tiny but healthy boys, we relished every inch of their perfectly named selves. I put those girl names on the shelf, assuming that if we had a daughter one day, we would bring one of them back down and use it.

Three and a half years later, I gave birth to a beautiful wide-eyed daughter, but my husband and I left the flowy, flowery names on the shelf. Whether it was because that pregnancy was fraught with problems or because we had changed enough in those few years to want meaning over sentimentality, we gave her a name that seemed to pick our girl rather than the other way around: Faith.

Simple. Classic. Meaningful. It would be our future grown-up daughter's reminder to grasp God always. It would be our own reminder to simply keep the simple things at the heart of life.

It would show this young mama how God uses change to rewrite our stories for the better.

When it all comes down to it, it's easy to *simply be* when you simply keep faith first. I say words from 2 Corinthians 5:7 under my breath: *I live by faith, not by sight.*

I live by faith.

I live by faith.

John 10:10 says the thief comes to steal and destroy, but Jesus comes so that we may have life to the full. I have spent much of life seeing change as the thief, but I now see Jesus in the change. Jesus means for us to have life to the full during changing times. I can obediently hold on to faith knowing that living life to the full is possible during all transitions.

I live by faith.

That faith is the light on the front porch of my heart's home. It's always on, always shining brightest in the darkest of night. The bulb may flicker out when stones of disbelief crack or damage it. But when it does, I regroup, remember, and replace it so it shines again. I reenter into Jesus's heart and ponder the words of St. Augustine: "Faith is to believe what you do not see; the reward of this faith is to see what you believe."[4]

My reward is seeing how I believe this God-reality: *change is just God's next step to my next best thing.*

I live by faith that he lives to give me the best no matter the season. No matter the current view. So I settle into the creaking rocker under the light on this wide front porch and watch the glowing, changing, star-bursting evening sky.

And the girl who met change smiles, because she likes what she sees.

Prayer

Dear Father God, thank you for the sincerest invitation to live in you and to make my home in you. Thank you for being the place of true rest where I am at home and held. May I know that no matter my season, no matter how I feel, I am always safe to enter in. May you be so alive in me that I feel safe to show you every messy corner of my heart. When change enters my life, may I allow your comfort to so fill me that I can't help but spill over and comfort other sisters going through transition too. May I simply be with you so my joy may be complete. I love you and am grateful for your never-changing, grace-slinging love. In the enduring name of Jesus, amen.

Conclusion

Changed by Change

When my sisters Megan and Sara and I were young, we ran wild on our corner of the Oklahoma prairie, and our choice playmates to run wild with were cousins who lived up and down the gravel lane by our house. If Jennifer and Emily would call us on our party line phone and ask if we could play, Mama would usually say yes. But before we tied up our tennis shoes and flew out the front door, Daddy would remind us of the familiar rule: "Make sure you stay close enough to hear me whistle. And when I whistle, girls, you need to come back home."

Daddy could whistle like a steam locomotive, and it hurt your ears if you were next to him when he let it go. Needless to say, his whistle still gave us a wide range of play places to roam. As long as we were near enough to hear it, we knew we weren't in trouble. We knew we were safe and close to home. So when Daddy whistled and it rode a breeze to our ears, we knew it was time to turn toward home.

I now think of that whistle when I consider change. I hear it ringing out and I know I'm still safely within range of God's care and provision. I see it as a sign to turn toward home, to turn toward Jesus.

So often I think of life as moving in a straight line. *Begin here, end there.* But it doesn't. It moves in circles. One ending taps a new beginning and says, "Tag, you're it!" That new beginning becomes a familiar middle and eventually finds an end of its own. It's another sign of change's natural rhythm, and it's one that's tagged me in that ending-turned-new-beginning once again.

When I met and married David as a young adult, change was the thing that took me away from the familiar. As I plant roots with my good man and growing kids, change *is* the thing that feels familiar.

For the past few years, we have made our home under the clear azure skies of Colorado, and it seems this state bound in place by mountains and covered in the warmth of frequent sunshine is shaping up to be a more long-term home for my family. As a woman who has spent the last twenty years in constant change, I am surprised that the prospect of staying put brings a whole new kind of change, such as:

Relearning my role as a wife, one that looks different with my less-often-traveling husband's more frequent presence.

Allowing my local church and friends to see the deeper, more real me that shorter stays don't always afford.

Allowing my maxi-dress-wearing, warm-weather-loving self to feel at home in a wool-coat-required, snow-blanketed climate.

Seeking contentment in the familiar places of here rather than waiting for the excitement of a new location to bring it to me.

Yeah, it's funny how *not* changing can be a change too. But even in the not changing there is certain truth: if God is close in the change that comes *to* us, then he is working to bring out some positive change *in* us as well.

I want to have my movement throughout my day reflect what my mind and heart know: that change is good and not something to dread. I want to live this truth revealed rather than concealed. There is a lightness, an attractiveness in the woman who is able to live like what she knows is true *actually is true*. Her spirit is then free to move beyond just embracing change to changing the world. Ann Voskamp says, "We get to change the world—every time we choose to change personally. We get to change the world every time we choose to have a heart change."[1]

I've had a heart change about change, and my prayer is you have too. I pray that as women wanting a genuine God-for-Kristen and God-for-Alycia and God-for-Brandi and God-for-Jeana and God-for-*you* story, we don't want to just settle into our own happy places where we're friends with change. We want to use this change as a vehicle to travel to our own little mission fields. So we join hands and hearts with other change-detesters-turned-faith-embracers to create a movement of people who don't run like scaredy-cats from the transitions in our lives but give ourselves permission to feel the way change will unfold from the outside and the inside. We know we don't have to *just get over it* but keep honest communication open with God and others so we can instead just get *through* it. We believe it's perfectly acceptable to go ahead and give up as we hold on to a flexible spirit. We accept the limitations our change brings and see them as invitations to live well rather than excuses to sit in misery. We understand that when change plants us in a windowless room, gratitude gives us a window to welcome the light so we don't wander in the dark. We believe that instead of wringing our hands because of change, we can infuse prayer with God's Word and simultaneously wield a sword at our fears. We know to huddle in close together and allow our friends to serve us as we serve them. We know how to ask the right questions during change so we are most aware of God's purposes.

> *During all seasons of life, we know that because we are alive in Christ and he is alive in us, we are held and at home.*

And above all, during all seasons of life, we know that because we are alive in Christ and he is alive in us, we are held and at home.

What's more, we will keep a faith embrace as the central core of our way of life. A faith embrace is what Abraham did when he willingly and obediently entered into God's plans for his change. A faith embrace is what Joseph did when he made several small but wise decisions to behave in accordance with God's unseen promises rather than the seen changes in his circumstances. A faith embrace is what Esther held on to by risking death to do right by her people. A faith embrace is what Allison did by turning over her son's future to her Father rather than clinging to familiar lies about it. A faith embrace is what Sherri did when she put her trust in God's acceptance of her rather than her husband's. A faith embrace is what Cheryl did when she and her husband stepped into a less secure, less comfortable future because God's will felt like the only secure, comfortable place to be. A faith embrace is what

Aundrea did when she traded her unanswered questions for her faith in God's plans.

A faith embrace is what I do when I wonder where God plans to send our family next, literally and figuratively. A faith embrace is what you do when you let your actions be determined by what God says he will do rather than on what you know you can't do (see Rom. 4:17 The Message).

A faith embrace is what we all can do when we embrace trust in God rather than trust in ourselves.

And when we ourselves are filled to overflowing with the love of that embrace, we are in a position to deliver fruit and blessings to our family members, friends, Bible study gals, PTO moms, co-workers, community members, and sister-friends over backyard fences and faraway oceans.

> By entering through faith into what God has always wanted to do for us—set us right with him, make us fit for him—we have it all together with God because of our Master Jesus. And that's not all: We throw open our doors to God and discover at the same moment that he has already thrown open his door to us. We find ourselves standing where we always hoped we might stand— out in the wide open spaces of God's grace and glory, standing tall and shouting our praise. (Romans 5:1–2 The Message)

Change doesn't take away God's wide-open spaces of grace and glory; it is one kind of setting for it.

Clothed in a fresh idea of change, we hold out our hands and ask God to bring blessings from it so we may be a blessing to others. We accept that God pours blessings on us so we can be the blessing he gives away. We say out loud, "Lord, seeing change differently has changed me. What can I do now?" We ask him to change our vision so our eyes are wide open to the lonely, the forgotten, the least loved. We ask him to change our plans so we are best equipped to be his tool for changing the lives of others he puts in our path.

As with Abraham, God's purpose in blessing one is to bless many, and he brings change to one so she may change many for the better. Yes, change always brings God's invitation to believe his familiar promises. He says to us, "This new change comes with my same promise of blessing. Accept that this change is a grace, not a grievance. Let your heart rest at home in me, thriving in the knowledge that I'm always looking out for your next best thing."

When these truths securely fix themselves to my heart, I find it's possible to thrive right here in my strategically placed and divinely chosen home.

Change is a helper—believe it.

Change is a gift—receive it.

Change is a restorer—live it.

Bible Truths That Never Change

Here are a few Bible verses that provide rock-solid support during times of change:

> The Lord is good to those whose hope is in him,
> to the one who seeks him.
>
> Lamentations 3:25

> Teach me knowledge and good judgment,
>   for I trust your commands.
>
> Psalm 119:66

> The Spirit of the Sovereign Lord is on me,
>   because the Lord has anointed me
>   to proclaim good news to the poor.

He has sent me to bind up the brokenhearted,
 to proclaim freedom for the captives
 and release from darkness for the prisoners,
to proclaim the year of the LORD's favor
 and the day of vengeance of our God,
to comfort all who mourn,
 and provide for those who grieve in Zion—
to bestow on them a crown of beauty
 instead of ashes,
the oil of joy
 instead of mourning,
and a garment of praise
 instead of a spirit of despair.
They will be called oaks of righteousness,
 a planting of the LORD
 for the display of his splendor.

          Isaiah 61:1–3

Come with me by yourselves to a quiet place and get some rest. (Mark 6:31)

I have come into the world as a light, so that no one who believes in me should stay in darkness. (John 12:46)

I have told you now before it happens, so that when it does happen you will believe. (John 14:29)

Abraham "believed God, and it was credited to him as righteousness." Understand, then, that those who have faith are children of Abraham. Scripture foresaw that God would justify the Gentiles by faith, and announced the gospel in advance to Abraham: "All nations will be blessed through you." So those who rely on faith are blessed along with Abraham, the man of faith. (Gal. 3:6–9)

I pray that the eyes of your heart may be enlightened in order that you may know the hope to which he has called you, the riches of his glorious inheritance in his holy people, and his incomparably great power for us who believe. (Eph. 1:18–19)

For this reason I kneel before the Father, from whom his every family in heaven and on earth derives its name. I pray that out of his glorious riches he may strengthen you with power through his Spirit in your inner being, so that Christ may dwell in your hearts through faith. And I pray that you, being rooted and established in love, may have power, together with all the Lord's holy people, to grasp how wide and long and high and deep is the love of Christ. (Eph. 3:14–18)

We do not want you to become lazy, but to imitate those who through faith and patience inherit what has been promised. (Heb. 6:12)

Because of this oath, Jesus has become the guarantor of a better covenant. . . . Therefore he is able to save completely those who come to God through him, because he always lives to intercede for them. (Heb. 7:22, 25)

Be content with what you have, because God has said, "Never will I leave you; never will I forsake you." So we say with confidence, "The Lord is my helper; I will not be afraid. What can mere mortals do to me?" (Heb. 13:5–6)

Acknowledgments

Thank you, God, for seeing the dreams of a little girl and bringing them to life in your timing. And thank you, Jesus, for faithfully loving me through all life's changes.

David, I always tell you I don't deserve a husband as generous and good as you. But then nobody else does either, so I will just be happy you're mine! Thank you for having patience with me, a girl whose aversion to change was as wide as your affection for it. You never push me through life's seasons but always hold my hand as the most gracious, affirming partner. I am in awe of you and love you madly.

James, Ethan, and Faith, thank you for not once complaining as your sometimes cranky mama worked on this project. May you always know how unchanging my love for you is.

Mama, thank you for proofreading approximately 1,473 English papers during my growing up years and for always finding something kind to say about each one. I wouldn't be any kind of writer without your early help and encouragement.

Daddy, thank you for always telling me to "write what you know." This book is proof I listened! Thank you for always loving me like Jesus does.

Sara and Megan, thanks for being sisters who encourage well and love deep.

Dan and Bev, thank you for treating me like a daughter rather than a daughter-in-law. Your attention and interest not only in this project but also in my life makes me feel unbelievably loved and appreciated.

To those dear women who were kind and brave enough to let me include their personal stories, I thank you wholeheartedly. Stacey, Aundrea, Tsh, Sherri, Allison, Jen, Cheryl, Mary, and Becky, your contributions make this book sing.

To my extended family and friends who encouraged me in countless ways—especially Uncle Tim, Suzie, Libby, Keri, Erin, Sally, Emily, Jennifer, Felicia, Aimée, and the entire Cornerstone Community of Village Seven Presbyterian—thank you for spurring me on.

Allison Crumpton, years ago you wrote a text saying this book would happen. Thank you for being my top *when* person and a true-blue friend.

Cheryl Clanahan, your words always walk through the front door of my heart at just the right time. Thank you for never failing to encourage me at the very moment I need it most.

Rebecca and Ryan Petersen, thank you for your constant hope-filled outlook about the words in these pages. And above all, thank you for being our favorite "framily."

Lana Elings, thank you for not batting an eye when you came home and found me typing away in your empty house. You are a gift.

To the Juniper Court girlfriends—specifically Rebecca, Cheryl, Jen, Mary, Lisa, Elisabeth, Tricia, Suzanna, Amy, and Becky—you are living proof of the abundance God brings by way of change. I hope we can be neighbors again in heaven.

Holley Gerth, thank you for constantly seeing things in me I can't see in myself. You are equal parts heart surgeon and heart sister, and I adore you.

Emily Freeman, you are the best kind of writing mentor and friend. Thank you for loving me and encouraging me through this journey and for never treating me like the clueless girl I am. You will always be one of my favorite writers.

Jennifer Dukes Lee, Lisa-Jo Baker, Robin Dance, Crystal Stine, Ann Voskamp, Dawn Camp, Melissa Michaels, Nish Weiseth, and Tsh Oxenreider, thank you, gracious friends, for cheering me on with the gift of your words and your knees. Your hearts are as big as your talent, and I love you.

To the writers of (in)courage and the DaySpring team, thank you for being more family than friends. You are smart, gracious, and kind, and you're the best encouragers and creators on the 'net.

Myquillyn Smith, I can never thank you enough for writing the foreword for this book. You are gloriously gifted and crazy generous, and I couldn't be more thrilled to have your name next to mine on this book's cover.

To Ruth Samsel, thank you for choosing me, encouraging me, and making me a better, more thoughtful writer. I will love you forever.

To the flat-out amazing Andrea Doering and the gifted Revell team including Twila Bennett, Wendy Wetzel, and Michele Misiak. Y'all are not only God's gift to publishing

but also God's gift to me. Thank you for believing in this book
. . . and in me. I adore y'all somethin' fierce.

To my readers at *Chasing Blue Skies*, thinking of you makes
me smile and sing. Thank you for your encouragement, interest, and prayers as I scrawled out this book. And thank you
for meeting up with me on the front porch of my blog. You're
my kind of people, and I love you to pieces.

Notes

Chapter 3 Don't Just Get Over It

1. Stacey Thacker, "When the View from Where You Sit Is Rather Grey," *29 Lincoln Avenue* (blog), April 9, 2014, http://www.29lincolnavenue.com/2014/04/when-the-view-from-where-you-sit-is-rather-grey/. Accessed March 13, 2015.

2. *A Lexicon: Abridged from Liddell and Scott's Greek-English* (Oxford, England: Oxford University Press, 1891; 1980).

3. See D. A. Carson, *The Gospel According to John*, Pillar New Testament Commentary (Grand Rapids: Eerdmans, 1991), and Tim Keller, "Truth, Tears, Anger, and Grace (John 11:20-53)," sermon text available in *Journal of Biblical Counseling* 20 no. 1, http://www.cccf.org/truth-tears-anger-and-grace-john-1120-53.

4. Aundrea's story is taken from personal conversations and emails with the author. Used by permission.

Chapter 4 Go Ahead and Give Up

1. Emily Freeman, "The Sacred Work of Sitting," *Chatting at the Sky* (blog), May 15, 2014, http://www.chattingatthesky.com/2014/05/15/sacred-work-sitting.

2. Holley Gerth, *You're Going to Be Okay: Encouraging Truth Your Heart Needs to Hear, Especially on the Hard Days* (Grand Rapids: Revell, 2014), 50–51.

3. Ibid., 54.

4. Theodore Roosevelt, *The Works of Theodore Roosevelt: History as Literature and Other Essays* (New York: Scribner, 1913), 303–4.

5. James Strong, *The New Strong's Exhaustive Concordance of the Bible* (Nashville: Thomas Nelson, 1990), 86.

6. Jeff A. Benner, "Ancient Hebrew Word Meanings," *Ancient Hebrew Research Center,* http://www.ancient-hebrew.org/27_eternity.html. Accessed September 10, 2014.

7. *Strong's Concordance,* "2617a. chesed," Bible Hub, http://biblehub.com/hebrew/2617a.htm. Accessed September 10, 2014.

8. "Survivor: South Pacific—Immunity Challenge Coconut Conundrum," YouTube video, 8:16, clip from *Survivor: South Pacific,* posted by CBS, September 14, 2011, https://www.youtube.com/watch?v=olPiw u-VDuA.

9. Beth Moore, *The Patriarchs: Encountering the God of Abraham, Isaac, and Jacob* (Nashville: Lifeway, 2005), 15.

Chapter 5 Accepting Limitations

1. Tsh Oxenreider, "Pop Goes the Bum Knee," *(in)courage* (blog), March 8, 2013, http://www.incourage.me/2013/03/pop-goes-the-bum-knee.html.

2. Myquillyn Smith, *The Nesting Place: It Doesn't Have to Be Perfect to Be Beautiful* (Grand Rapids: Zondervan, 2014), 101.

3. Ibid., 102.

4. Max Lucado, *You'll Get through This: Hope and Help for Your Turbulent Times* (Nashville: Thomas Nelson, 2013), 51.

5. Arthur Gordon, *A Touch of Wonder* (Old Tappan, NJ: Revell, 1995), 213.

Chapter 6 Light in a Windowless Room

1. Corrie ten Boom, *The Hiding Place* (Grand Rapids: Chosen, 2006), 209.

2. Ann Voskamp, *One Thousand Gifts* (Grand Rapids: Zondervan, 2014), 36.

3. Ibid., 35.

4. Douglas Harper, *Online Etymology Dictionary,* s.v. "optimism," accessed February 6, 2015, http://www.etymonline.com/index.php?term=optimism &allowed_in_frame=0.

5. Matthew Henry, *Matthew Henry's Commentary on the Whole Bible: Complete and Unabridged in One Volume* (Peabody, MA: Hendrickson, 1994).

6. Ibid.

7. Dietrich Bonhoeffer, *Life Together* (New York: Harper & Row, 1954), 29.

Chapter 7 Handing Over the Hand-Wringing

1. Robert Boyd Munger, *My Heart—Christ's Home* (Madison, WI: InterVarsity Press, 1954), 15–16.

2. Annie Dillard, *Teaching a Stone to Talk: Expeditions and Encounters* (New York: Harper Collins, 2009), 52.

Chapter 8 Because We All Need Friends in Low Places

1. Lily Koppel, *The Astronaut Wives Club* (New York: Grand Central, 2014), 279.
2. Bonhoeffer, *Life Together*, 20.
3. Lysa TerKeurst, *The Best Yes: Making Wise Decisions in the Midst of Endless Demands* (Nashville: Thomas Nelson, 2014), 11.
4. Bonhoeffer, *Life Together*, 21.

Chapter 9 Asking the Right Questions to Become Fit for the Right Purpose

1. S.v. "adapt," WordNet Dictionary, http://www.webster-dictionary.org/definition/adapt. Accessed March 15, 2015.
2. Robert Browning, "A Pillar at Sebzevar," *The Works of Robert Browning* (Hertfordshire, UK: Wordsworth Ed. Limited, 1994).

Chapter 10 Settling in the Home Where Your Heart Thrives

1. Julie Perkins Cantrell, "Home Filled with Love," *Julie Cantrell* (blog), July 7, 2010, https://juliecantrell.wordpress.com/2010/07/07/home-filled-with-love/.
2. Munger, *My Heart—Christ's Home*, 26–28.
3. Jean Fleming, *Pursue the Intentional Life* (Colorado Springs: NavPress, 2013), 76.
4. Augustine of Hippo, Sermones 4.1.1., quoted at http://en.wikiquote.org/wiki/Faith.

Conclusion

1. Ann Voskamp, "How Your Life Really Can Change (and What to Do When Change Comes)," *A Holy Experience* (blog), http://www.aholyexperience.com/2014/07/how-your-life-really-can-change-and-what-to-do-when-it-does/.

Kristen Strong was born and raised in Oklahoma but has since traveled far and wide with her air force family. As the wife of a career veteran, she speaks from the heart of a woman who has experienced change in many makes and models. You can read more of Kristen's writing at her blog *Chasing Blue Skies* (www.chasingblueskies.net) and at (in)courage (www. incourage.me), the blog of DaySpring. She has penned contributions for *MOMSense* and *Family Fun* magazines.

Kristen and her husband, David, have three delightful children and enjoy their current home under the wide blue skies of Colorado.

Connect with Kristen

Chasing Blue Skies

Kristen_Strong

kristenstrong

Kristen Strong